THE MOST
TRUSTED NAME
IN **TRAVEL**

Shortcut
ANDALUCIA

by Patricia Harris and David Lyon

FrommerMedia LLC

Published by
Frommer Media LLC

Copyright © 2015 by Frommer Media LLC. All rights reserved. No part of this publication may be reproduced, stored in a retrieval system, or transmitted in any form or by any means, electronic, mechanical, photocopying, recording, scanning or otherwise, except as permitted under Sections 107 or 108 of the 1976 United States Copyright Act, without the prior written permission of the Publisher. Requests to the Publisher for permission should be addressed to: Support@FrommerMedia. com. Frommer's is a registered trademark of Arthur Frommer. Frommer Media LLC is not associated with any product or vendor mentioned in this book.

ISBN 978-1-62887-216-3 (paper), 978-1-62887-217-0 (e-book)

Editorial Director: Pauline Frommer
Editor: Anuja Madar
Production Editor: Lynn Northrup
Cartographer: Liz Puhl
Photo Editor: Dana Davis

For information on our other products or services, see www.frommers.com.

Frommer Media LLC also publishes its books in a variety of electronic formats. Some content that appears in print may not be available in electronic formats.

Manufactured in China

5 4 3 2 1

FROMMER'S STAR RATINGS SYSTEM

Every hotel, restaurant, and attraction listed in this guide has been ranked for quality and value. Here's what the stars mean:

★ Recommended
★★ Highly Recommended
★★★ A must! Don't miss!

AN IMPORTANT NOTE

The world is a dynamic place. Hotels change ownership, restaurants hike their prices, museums alter their opening hours, and busses and trains change their routings. And all of this can occur in the several months after our authors have visited, inspected, and written about, these hotels, restaurants, museums and transportation services. Though we have made valiant efforts to keep all our information fresh and up-to-date, some few changes can inevitably occur in the periods before a revised edition of this guidebook is published. So please bear with us if a tiny number of the details in this book have changed. Please also note that we have no responsibility or liability for any inaccuracy or errors or omissions, or for inconvenience, loss, damage, or expenses suffered by anyone as a result of assertions in this guide.

CONTENTS

LIST OF MAPS

ABOUT THE AUTHORS

Patricia Harris and **David Lyon** have journeyed the world for American, British, Swiss, and Asian publishers to write about food, culture, art, and design. They have covered subjects as diverse as elk migrations in western Canada, the street markets of Shanghai, winter hiking on the Jungfrau, and the origins of Mesoamerican civilization in the Mexican tropics. In the name of research, they have eaten hot-pepper-toasted grasshoppers, tangles of baby eels, and roasted armadillo in banana sauce. Wherever they go, they are repeatedly drawn back to Spain for the flamenco nightlife, the Moorish architecture of Andalucía, the world-weary and lust-ridden saints of Zurbarán, and the phantasmagoric visions of El Greco. They can usually be found conversing with the locals in neighborhood bars while drinking the house wine and eating patatas bravas and grilled shrimp with garlic. They are the co-authors of *Frommer's Spain Day by Day* and *Frommer's EasyGuide to Madrid and Barcelona*.

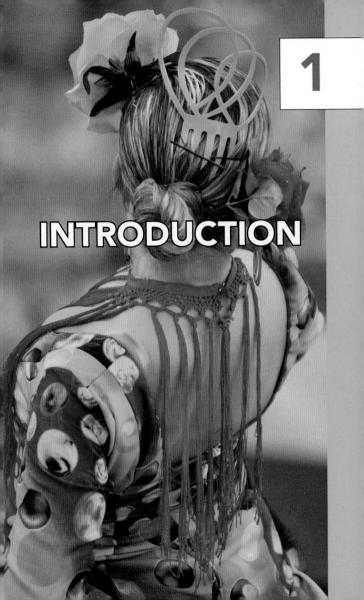

1

INTRODUCTION

Much of what the world imagines as Spain is, in fact, Andalucía. It was the cradle of flamenco, the stomping grounds of the amorous Don Juan, and the tragic setting for *Carmen*. It's the region where bulls are bred and matadors are more famous than rock stars. Nothing in Andalucía is done halfway. The flowers are brighter and the music is both more melancholy and more joyful. Although Andalucía is often a stand-in for Spain in the popular imagination, it was, in fact, the last stronghold of the Moors, who held al-Andalus for over 7 centuries. Consequently, Andalucía shines with all the medieval Muslim glories of Europe: the world-famous Mezquita (mosque) of Córdoba, the Alhambra Palace of Granada, and (in their own way as Christian-Muslim hybrids) Sevilla's imposing Alcázar and looming Gothic cathedral. Its smaller towns can be haunting in their beauty: the whitewashed mountain villages, the Renaissance grace of Ubeda, the drama of gorge-split Ronda, the languor of sherry-besotted Jerez de

PREVIOUS PAGE: **Flamenco dancer in Sevilla.**

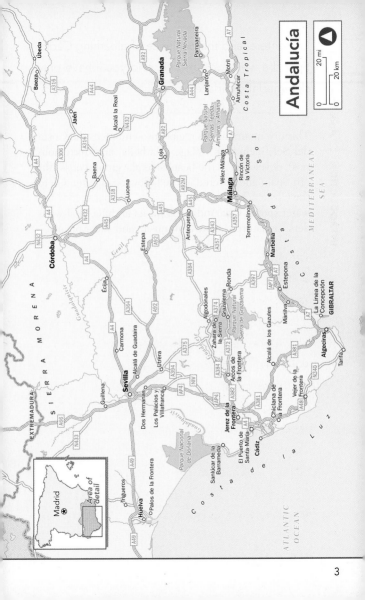

la Frontera, and the brilliance of gleaming Cádiz. Spend a week or a month, and you'll have only skimmed the surface.

This dry, mountainous region also embraces the Costa del Sol (including Málaga, Marbella, and Torremolinos), developed as the beachside playground of southern Spain and covered in the following chapter. Go to the Costa del Sol for beach resorts, the bar scene, and water sports; visit Andalucía for its architectural wonders, signature cuisine and music, and sheer beauty.

SEVILLA

2

Sevilla is Andalucía's largest, most self-assured, and most sophisticated city—the hometown of the passionate Carmen and the lusty Don Juan. Style matters here. Almost every Sevillana owns at least one flamenco dress to wear during the city's famous April *fería*—or to a friend or family member's wedding. It may also be the most ornately decorated city in Spain. No country does baroque like the Spanish, and no city does Spanish baroque like Sevilla, where the style represents the hybrid offspring of Moorish decoration and the Catholic insistence on turning every abstract curlicue of Islam into a Christian angel's wing. Sevilla has been Andalucía's center of power and influence since Fernando III of Castilla tossed out the Almohad rulers in 1248. But Fernando wisely left Barrio Santa Cruz intact, and the tangled ancient streets of the Judería still make the medieval era palpable. As the first major city in the heart of Andalucía to return to Spanish hands, Sevilla has a markedly Christian countenance. The city is studded with churches and

PREVIOUS PAGE: **Statuary in the Catedral de Sevilla.**

former convents funded by the riches that flowed into the city from its 16th to 18th century trade monopoly with the New World.

Essentials

GETTING THERE   Sevilla's **Aeropuerto San Pablo,** Calle Almirante Lobo (© **90-240-47-04;** www.aena-aeropuertos.es), is served by nearly two dozen airlines, including Iberia, Air Europa, Vueling, British Air, EasyJet, and Ryanair. The airport lies 9.6km (6 miles) from the center of the city, along the highway leading to Carmona. A bus run by **Transportes Urbanos de Sevilla** (© **90-245-99-54**) meets all incoming flights and transports you into the center of Sevilla for 4€.

Train service into Sevilla is centralized into the **Estación Santa Justa,** Av. Kansas City s/n (© **90-242-22-42;** www.renfe.com). Buses C1 and C2 take you from this train station to the bus station at Prado de San Sebastián, and bus EA runs to and from the airport. The high-speed AVE train has reduced travel time from Madrid to Sevilla to 2½ hours. The train makes 18 trips daily, with a stop in Córdoba, and costs 55€ to 86€. About three dozen trains daily connect Sevilla and Córdoba, taking from 45 minutes to 1¼ hours. Ten additional trains run to Málaga (2–2½ hr.) and four trains to Granada (3¼ hr.).

The new bus station at **Plaza de Armas** (© **95-490-80-40**) handles most long-distance bus traffic, while most buses within Andalucía use the **Prado de San Sebastián** terminal near Plaza de España, Calle Manuel Vazquez Sagastizabal, s/n. (© **95-441-71-11**). For information and ticket prices visit www.alsa.es.

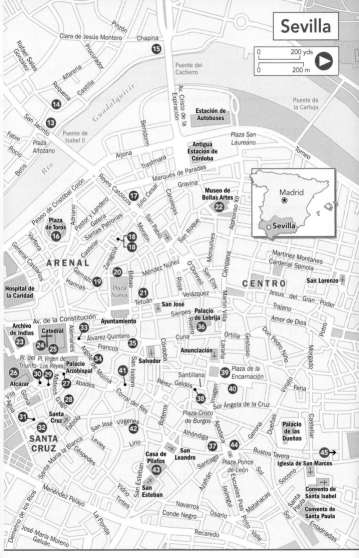

Sevilla is 549km (341 miles) southwest of Madrid and 217km (135 miles) northwest of Málaga. Several major highways converge on Sevilla, connecting it with the rest of Spain and Portugal. Sevilla is easy to drive to, but extremely difficult to drive around in (or to park).

GETTING AROUND   Don't even consider driving around Sevilla. If you give up a parking space you will never find another. Fortunately, the city is eminently walkable. If you need to get from one end to another in a hurry, hop an inexpensive bus (1.40€) instead of paying 10€ for a taxi. The city tram and Metro system is good for commuters but of little use to sightseers. The municipal bicycle rental program, **SEVICI,** provides access to bikes for a small subscription charge plus an even smaller hourly fee. The snazzy red bikes are parked in 250 areas all over the city, each with a kiosk where you can subscribe by credit card. A 1-week membership is 12€, and time fees range from 1.05€ to 2.05€ per hour (✆ **90-201-10-32;** www. sevici.es).

VISITOR INFORMATION   The tourist office, **Oficina de Información del Turismo,** at Plaza de San Francisco, 15 (Edificio Laredo; ✆ **95-459-52-88;** www. sevilla.org), is open Monday to Friday 9am to 7:30pm, Saturday 9:30am to 7:30pm, and Sunday 9:30am to 3pm.

SPECIAL EVENTS   The most popular times to visit Sevilla are during the **April Fair**—the most famous *feria* in Spain—and during **Holy Week (Semana Santa),** when religious floats called *pasos* are carried through the streets by robed penitents. Book lodging far in advance for both.

FAST FACTS　　There's a **U.S. consulate** at Plaza Nueva, 8 (✆ **95-421-87-51**), open Monday to Friday 11am to 1pm. For **medical emergencies,** go to the Hospital Virgen del Rocío, Av. Manuel Siurot s/n (✆ **95-501-20-00**), about 2km (1¼ miles) from the city center.

　　If you need a **cab,** call **Tele Taxi** (✆ **95-462-22-22**) or **Radio Taxi** (✆ **95-458-36-05**). Cabs are metered and charge a 2.66€ pickup fee by day, 3.34€ at night. Rates are 0.66€/km by day, 0.81€/km at night.

Where to Stay

If you choose lodging near the cathedral, the bells may jar you awake. Locals who grew up nearby claim they never notice the sound, and it's true that most visitors become accustomed to them quickly. During Semana Santa and *feria*, hotels double or even triple their rates, with increases often announced at the last minute. If you're going to be in Sevilla at these times, arrive with an ironclad reservation and an agreed price before checking in.

EXPENSIVE

Casa Número 7 ★★　　You could walk right past this tiny boutique hotel in Barrio Santa Ana and never realize the delights that lie behind its unpresuming facade. This 19th-century mansion features just six tastefully decorated rooms that represent a relaxed version of Spanish hacienda style. The hotel is intended as a place of rest, and it may be in the quietest location in an otherwise noisy city. There is strong Wi-Fi, but there are no televisions. Rooms are named by their dominant decorating color and range from the spacious Yellow Room, which has a balcony opening onto the street, to the snug Blue Room, with just one large bed instead of two. All have sumptuous marble baths.

Calle Vírgenes, 7. © **95-422-15-81.** www.casanumero7.com. 6 rooms. 130€–177€ double. Bus: 10, 15, 24, or 32. **Amenities:** Bar; free Wi-Fi.

Hotel Alfonso XIII ★★   Designed to be the model of decadent opulence, this neo-Mudéjar fantasy was built as the most luxurious hotel for the 1929 Exposición Iberoamericana. For generations it was the most exclusive address in Sevilla, and since the complete renovation for the Starwoods Luxury Collection was completed in 2013, the leather upholstery on the chairs is again buttery soft, the gilt-paint highlights and hand-painted tiles gleam, and the rich earth tones of the walls, carpets, and draperies conjure a palace from some land distant. The Alfonso XIII boasts old-fashioned service with 21st-century plumbing and wireless technology.
Calle San Fernando, 2. © **800/325-3589** in the U.S. and Canada, or 95-491-70-00. www.hotel-alfonsoxiii-seville.com. 147 units. 209€–409€ double; from 359€ jr. suite; from 459€ suite. Parking 20€. Bus: 10 or 15. **Amenities:** 2 restaurants; 3 bars; concierge; exercise room; outdoor pool; outdoor tennis court (lit); Wi-Fi for a fee.

Hotel Casa 1800 ★★   This charming boutique hotel steps from the cathedral occupies an 1864 limestone mansion built for the mayor of Sevilla. After 3 years of renovation to preserve its historic details, it opened as a hotel in spring 2011. Many rooms have exposed beams from the original structure and the original plaster-on-stone walls were retained wherever possible. The hotel is filled with original art, giving it the gracious air of a private manse. The decor is luxe—tufted ottomans, overhead chandeliers, beds with artistic and elaborate headboards, and parquet wood floors. The rooftop terrace has stunning views of the Alcázar and the cathedral. Room 302 on the terrace level has a private terrace and is the most requested room in the house. It is one of three deluxe rooms with a terrace and Jacuzzi tub.

Calle Rodrigo Caro, 6. ✆ **95-456-18-00.** www.hotelcasa1800. com. 24 rooms. 130€–230€ double. Bus: T1, C5. **Amenities:** Restaurant; 2 bars; concierge; free Wi-Fi.

MODERATE

El Rey Moro Hotel ★★ Created in 2009 from a 16th-century manor house built around a patio with an 8th-century Moorish fountain, the family-run El Rey Moro spans the centuries with colorful contemporary rooms inspired by historic design motifs. Wall colors are warm and intense, and the furnishings tend to be quirky, one-of-a-kind pieces. The rooms are arrayed on two levels around the central courtyard, and many of them retain the old plaster walls and exposed ceiling beams of the original house. This corner of Barrio Santa Cruz is about a 4-minute walk from the cathedral. Guests have free use of house bicycles.

Calle Lope de Rueda, 14. ✆ **95-456-34-68.** www.elreymoro. com. 19 rooms. 79€–189€ double. Bus: T1, C5. **Amenities:** Restaurant; free Wi-Fi.

Hotel Bécquer ★ The palace of the Marquès de Los Torres was converted into this grand hotel in the 1970s, with some antiques saved from the old building. Only two blocks from the Río Guadalquivír, it's close to the Puente Isabel II for walking into Triana, and not far from the bullring, but for other sights you'll likely need to take a taxi. Rooms are small, low-key, and modern, with either two twins or one double bed. Guests who book through the hotel website get a laptop, PlayStation, and iPad to use onsite.

Calle Reyes Católicos, 4. ✆ **95-422-89-00.** www.hotelbecquer. com. 141 units. 73€–161€ double. Parking 15€. Bus: C1, C2, or

C4. **Amenities:** Restaurant; 2 bars; rooftop pool; spa; free Wi-Fi.

Hotel Doña María ★★   You can never be too close to the centers of power. No doubt that's what Samuel Levi thought when he had his 14th-century in-town palace built here next to the Alcázar so that he could pop in to advise Pedro the Cruel. (Legend holds that there were once underground passageways between the buildings.) By the late 19th century, the structure belonged to the Marquises de Pena, who gave it the current facade for the 1929 Exposición Iberoamerica. In 1965, the Marquise de San Joaquín turned the palace into a hotel, making her Sevilla's first woman hotelier. Alterations over the years have carved out rooms in different shapes and sizes, so ask to move if you're unhappy with what you get. The vast lobby area and hallways are filled with Spanish antiques and old paintings. The rooftop terrace has a small pool, but most guests gravitate to the bar with its in-your-face views of the cathedral and La Giralda. The hotel has a relaxed, old-fashioned feel complemented by the warm and attentive service.
Calle Don Remondo, 19. ℂ **95-422-49-90.** www.hdmaria.com. 64 units. 75€–154€ double. Parking 20€. Bus: C1, C2, or C4. **Amenities**: 2 bars; outdoor pool; free Wi-Fi.

Hotel Inglaterra Sevilla ★   A frankly overdue renovation in 2012 restored this 1857 grande dame to its former glory while reconfiguring the spaces to create fewer, larger rooms. As the name suggests, the hotel emulates *el corte inglés*, the English style that inspired the name of the department store chain. Nowhere is it more evident than in the lounges and bars on the ground level, where the polished wood and the bottles of Scotch make you think that Winston

Churchill and his bulldog will come wandering out at any minute. Service here is gracious and old-fashioned. Rooms are fresh and simply decorated with brocaded floral fabrics in subdued gold tones and wooden chairs and headboards; the tile and marble baths all have contemporary fixtures. The Plaza Nueva location could not be more central.

Plaza Nueva, 7. ℂ **94-522-49-70.** www.hotelinglaterra.es. 86 rooms. 79€–184€ double. Bus: T1, C5. **Amenities:** Restaurant; 2 bars; concierge; free Wi-Fi.

Hotel Palace Sevilla ★   Opening onto Plaza de la Encarnación and the monumental "Las Setas" (p. 30, many rooms have views of it), this richly appointed small hotel opened in 2013. The decor references Sevilla's baroque tradition, especially in the swirling forms and heavy ruffles, yet it's all executed with a modern color palette that suggests whimsy rather than slavish imitation. Beds are big and plush and every room is equipped with state-of-the-art hydro-massage showers. Superior doubles even come with a laptop at the desk (though this line of rooms can be snug). The ground-level terrace is a bar, becoming a dinner restaurant in summer.

Plaza de la Encarnación, 17. ℂ **95-531-09-09.** www.hotelsevil lapalace.es. 34 rooms. 80€–145€ double. Bus: 27, 32, A2. **Amenities:** Bar; concierge; free Wi-Fi.

Hotel Palacio Alcázar ★   Located on a quiet, orange tree–filled plaza nearly touching the walls of the Alcázar, this breezy and modern boutique guest house occupies the former home and studio of American bullfighter and painter John Fulton. The days when he made it a crash pad for aspiring matadors are long gone, but the tiny property, which became a hotel in 2011, retains his sense of generous hospitality.

Bright impressionistic paintings cover the doors of all the units. Some units have small terraces, while the first-floor Room 3 has a small patio and a spiral staircase to a sleeping loft that could be used for children. Plaza de Allianza, 11. ✆ **95-450-21-90.** www.palacioalcazar. com. 12 rooms. 51€–150€ double. BusL T1. **Amenities:** Free Wi-Fi.

Hotel Ribera de Triana ★ On the Triana side of the Puente Cristo de la Expiración from the Plaza de Armas bus station, this sleekly modern hotel has sweeping views of the Río Guadalquivír from about half the rooms as well as the shared rooftop terrace. The exercise room, also on the roof, has a hot tub with city views. Designed for business travelers, the Ribera de Triana is an excellent buy for leisure travelers as rooms are larger and more modern than at most hotels. Plaza Chapina, s/n. ✆ **95-426-80-00.** www.hotelriberadetriana. com. 136 units. 74€–161€ double. Parking 16€. Bus: 170, 174, 176. **Amenities:** Restaurant; 2 bars; rooftop pool; spa; free Wi-Fi.

La Casa del Maestro ★ Named for the famed flamenco guitarist "Niño Ricardo" (1904–72) who lived and died in the house, this charming little hotel near Plaza de Encarnación is painted with intense, earthy colors. Lacking a restaurant or even an elevator, it is classified by the city as a one-star hotel, yet rivals many a three-star property for charm. The building is the classic three floors around a central courtyard. The street level includes a large lounge area (with computer corner) where you can get coffee and hang out. Rooms are snug but attractively decorated; most have two twin beds. Calle Niño Ricardo, 5. ✆ **95-450-00-06.** www.lacasadelmaestro. com. 10 rooms. 60€–160€ double. Bus: 27, 32, A2. **Amenities:** Free Wi-Fi.

Las Casas de los Mercaderes ★   Joining two city palaces around a classic Andalucían patio, this three-story boutique hotel is just far enough away from the cathedral to avoid the crowds yet close to almost everything you might want to see. Public areas are quite grand, with lots of pale marble and handsome antique-styled furniture. Guest rooms are cozier, with heavy draperies and marble floors. This hotel is very popular with Spanish families, who book clusters of small rooms at the end of a hallway. Views from the rooftop terrace include, of course, La Giralda.

Calle Alvarez Quintero 9–13. ✆ **95-422-58-58.** www.casasy palacios.com. 47 units. 78€–123€ double. Parking 22€ per day. Bus: 21, 23, 41, or 42. **Amenities:** 2 bars; free Wi-Fi.

INEXPENSIVE

Hotel Goya ★   With its tiled bathrooms, marble tile floors, and pale wooden furniture, the Hotel Goya may have a lot of hard surfaces, but the staff are warm and welcoming and the rooms, while small, are extremely well designed. It's hard to imagine a better bargain lodging in the city, as everything is kept fresh and functional. The location is also very good for walking to the city sites. The hotel sits in the heart of the oldest part of Barrio de Santa Cruz, no more than a 5-minute stroll from the cathedral. Ask for an interior room off the courtyard in the back to avoid street noise.

Calle Mateus Gago, 31. ✆ **95-421-11-70.** www.hostalgoya sevilla.com. 19 units. 55€–95€ double. Bus: 10, 12, 41, or 42. **Amenities:** Free Wi-Fi.

Hotel Itaca Sevilla ★   Installed in a former private mansion, this handsome hotel opened in 2011 on a quiet street on the south side of Plaza de la Encarnación. Rooms circle a pretty courtyard and all have

17

exterior views through well-soundproofed windows. Modern, dark wood furniture with colorful upholstery, walls painted in warm tones, and crisp white linens give all the rooms a contemporary yet timeless air. Rooms tend to be small, but well designed to make maximum use of the space. You get a lot of style for the price.

Calle Santillana, 5. © **95-422-81-56.** www.itacasevilla. 23 rooms. 55€–95€ double. Bus: 27, 32, A2. **Amenities:** Free Wi-Fi.

Where to Eat

The North African influence on Sevilla cuisine is obvious in the honey-sweetened pastries and the abundant dates, almonds, saffron, and lemons. Gazpacho was made here with almonds and garlic long before tomatoes arrived from the New World, and breads are still baked in ancient ovens.

EXPENSIVE

Egaña Oriza ★★★ BASQUE/SPANISH Long one of the most elegant haute-cuisine restaurants in Sevilla, Egaña Oriza broadened its appeal in 2010 to include a tapas bar where you can still enjoy the creative cooking of Basque-born chef José Mari Egaña in a casual and less expensive format. (Most tapas are under 4€, and the tapa of the day with a beer or glass of wine is just 3.60€.) The more refined dining room is a model of white linens and crystal glassware, set inside the glassed-over courtyard of a historic mansion next to the Jardins de Murillo. Egaña has simplified his cuisine over the years, adding such dishes as a pappardelle carbonara with caviar (a first course) to Basque classics like hake with fried garlic or his wild boar stew with homemade quince compote.

Calle San Fernando, 41. ☎ **95-422-72-54.** www.restaurante oriza.com. Main courses 14€–28€; daily menu 45€. Mon–Sat 1:30–3:30pm and 8:30–11:30pm. Bus: 21 or 23. Closed Aug.

Taberna del Alabardero ★★ ANDALUCIAN

The upstairs dining rooms of this elegant town house near the Plaza de Toros have earned a reputation as one of the finest upscale restaurants in Sevilla. But it's frankly more fun to eat off the bistro menu in the downstairs tile-encrusted dining room that adjoins the central atrium cafe. The dishes are less precious, and everything is prepared and served by the faculty and students of the hotel and hospitality school, started here many years ago by a priest looking for a way to give street kids some marketable skills. The dishes are rib-stickers: the hearty potato and sausage stew known as Riojanas, cod *a pil pil* served with ratatouille topped with a poached egg, duck in Sevilla orange sauce, and rice pudding with a side of profiteroles. The restored mansion also serves as an inn, with seven spacious and elegant guest rooms.

Calle Zaragoza, 20. ☎ **95-450-27-21.** www.tabernadel alabardero.es. Reservations recommended. Main courses 19€–32€; 3-course bistro menu 13€ weekdays, 18€ weekends. Daily 1:30–4:30pm and 8:30pm–midnight. Inn: 7 rooms. 110€–150€ double; 150€–200€ junior suite. Bus: 21, 25, 30, or 43. Restaurant closed Aug.

MODERATE

Enrique Becerra ★ ANDALUCIAN

The upstairs dining room at this establishment just one street off Plaza Nueva serves excellent grilled meat and fish, but it's frankly too quiet. Everyone prefers to crowd into the bar and adjacent dining room on the ground floor to enjoy creative tapas—soft-cooked foie gras on toast, finger rolls stuffed with spicy steamed mussels, lamb meatballs in mint sauce, or cod in a pasta sack with almond-garlic sauce. The 35 sherries by the glass are very reasonably priced.

Calle Gamazo, 2. ℂ **95-421-30-49.** www.enriquebecerra.com. Tapas 3€–4€; *raciones* 6€–13€; main courses in restaurant 12€–22€. Mon–Sat 1–4:30pm and 8pm–midnight (closed Sat July–Aug). Bus: 21, 25, 30, or 40.

Barbiana ★★ ANDALUCIAN/SEAFOOD   If you've ever tasted the Manzanilla Barbiana from Sanlúcar de Barrameda, you already know what kind of food to expect at this related restaurant planted next to Plaza Nueva. Tangy and yeasty, with a hint of green almonds, it's a perfect complement to fish from the Huelva coast and crustaceans from Sanlúcar itself, and that's exactly what Barbiana serves. The kitchen offers mixed seafood with rice (*not* paella) at midday but not in the evening, when the volume of diners steers the menu toward quicker preparations like *tortillitas de camarones*, a fried batter of chickpea flour with tiny whole shrimp, or grilled rockfish (*sargo*) on garlicky red peppers.

Calle Albareda, 11. ℂ **95-422-44-02.** www.restaurantebarbiana. com. Reservations recommended. Main courses 9€–27€. Mon–Sat noon–5pm and 8pm–midnight. Bus: 21, 25, 30, or 40.

Casa Cuesta ★ ANDALUCIAN   Right across a small plaza from the Mercado de Triana, this historic tapas bar and drinking place of fishermen and bull-fighters still boasts the checkerboard marble floors and ornate polished bar of its late 19th-century origins. Known for salty classics such as *jamón serrano*, triangles of Manchego cheese, and potato salad with lots of garlic, Casa Cuesta is also acclaimed for its *flamequines*. They consist of a piece of pork sirloin wrapped in *jamón serrano*, battered, and deep-fried. They make you thirsty for another beer, which is the point.

Calle Castilla 1, Triana. ℗ **95-433-33-35.** www.casacuesta.net. Tapas 3€–5€; larger plates 7€–19€. Daily noon–midnight. Bus: B2 or 43.

Mesón Don Raimundo ★ ANDALUCIAN You can enjoy the trappings of history when you eat at this formal and classic restaurant in Barrio de Santa Cruz. Originally a Jewish residence, it was converted to a convent in 1362 and served as Sevilla's first post office in the 19th century. The dining rooms are elegant spaces with high-coffered ceilings and moody historic paintings on the walls. The food, we're happy to report, is brighter, more boisterous, and full of flavor. The combination of sweet and savory is typical of Sevillano Mozarabic cooking. Look for it in the venison stew, or the pheasant braised with apples. One of the restaurant's signature seafood dishes is the casserole of squid, grapes, and small fish.

Calle Argote de Molina, 26. ℗ **95-422-33-55.** www.mesondon raimundo.com. Reservations recommended. Main courses 15€–26€. Daily noon–4pm and 7:30pm–midnight. Bus: 21, 23, or 25.

INEXPENSIVE

Bodeguita Casablanca ★★★ ANDALUCIAN Established in 2005, this little corner bar near the Puerta de Jerez run by Tomás and Antonio Casablanca is justly acclaimed for the kitchen's deft riffs on traditional dishes. The Casablancas convert the humble *tortilla Española* into the noble Tortilla al Whisky, copied by chefs all over Spain. (The sauce is carefully cooked so the alcohol from the Scotch is retained.) In deference to the burger craze, the brothers created a radically Spanish version: two salt cod sliders served on a puddle of melted cheese. Most diners graze on tapas, but Casablanca also offers full plates, including a huge roast leg of lamb.

Calle Adolfo Rodríguez Jurado, 12. ✆ **95-422-41-14.** www.
bodeguitacasablanca.com. Tapas 2.50€; plates 12€–20€. Mon–
Fri 7am–5pm and 8:15pm–12:30am, Sat 12:30–5:30pm. Bus: T1.
Closed Sat-Sun in July, closed August.

El Rinconcillo ★ ANDALUCIAN   El Rinconcillo
was established in 1670 on a small street east of Plaza
de Encarnación. It was no doubt updated sometime in
the last 3-plus centuries, but not recently—which is,
of course, its charm. The latest additions to the decor
were the Art Nouveau tile murals installed sometime
in the late 19th or early 20th century. The lights are
dim, and hams and sausage dangle from the heavily
beamed ceilings. Good luck scoring one of the marble-
topped tables. We usually stand at the bar where the
bartender runs our tab in chalk. Some of the most
famous tapas are the house *croquetas* and the casserole of chickpeas and spinach.

Calle Gerona, 42. ✆ **95-422-31-83.** www.elrinconcillo.es.
Tapas 2.50€–3.50€; plates 9€–18€; set menus 26€–39€. Thurs–
Tues 1pm–1:30am. Bus: 12, 27, 32, A2, C5.

Restaurante Las Escobas ★ ANDALUCIAN/
CASTILIAN   When Cervantes ate here in the late
16th century, he called Las Escobas a *taberna antigua,*
since it had already been around since 1386. That
makes it (probably) the oldest eating establishment in
Europe. Las Escobas has been in the hands of its current owners for more than 40 years. Of all the restaurants on and just off the cathedral square, we feel this
spot gives the best value for the money and does the
best job preparing traditional cuisine.

Calle Alvarez Quintero, 62. ✆ **95-456-04-16.** www.lasescobas.
com. Tapas 2.80€; main courses 11€–17€; daily menu 16€;
tasting menu 44€. Daily noon–midnight. Bus: C5.

RIVERSIDE MEALS WITH A view

Possibly the most scenic overviews of Sevilla are from the Triana side of the Guadalquivír opposite the Torre del Oro. Two dining establishments serve on patios overlooking the river. They're literally next to each other, yet their only similarity is the view. The **Kiosco de las Flores** (Calle Betis, s/n; 𝄃 95-427-45-76; www.kioscodelasflores.com) is a casual fried-fish spot with a large menu that most diners ignore, preferring to order a bottle of wine (10€–20€) and cod, hake, or monkfish battered fish "bites." Main dishes are 8€ to 20€. It's open Tuesday to Saturday noon to 4pm and 8pm to midnight, Sunday noon to 4pm. The hyper-elegant **Abades Triana** (Calle Betis, s/n; 𝄃 95-428-64-59; www.abadestriana.com) is often booked solid for weddings because both the setting and the restaurant are so beautiful. But avoid summer Saturdays, and you can treat yourself to the caviar menu or enjoy contemporary, somewhat lightened preparations of roasted fish and meat, followed by one of the fancy desserts (cheese, strawberries, and caramel, for example). Main dishes are 19€ to 29€. Menus range from 35€ for the business lunch to 80€ for the tasting menu. It's open Tuesday to Saturday noon to 4pm and 8 to 11pm, Sunday noon to 5pm. Both restaurants can be reached by buses C3, 5, 40, and 41.

Exploring Sevilla

A city of 1.7 million people, Sevilla sprawls in every direction from its historic heart. A Metro system is under construction to speed up getting around, but to date it is of little help in the old city. To see the sights, plan to walk. The cathedral and the Alcázar anchor one end of the city, with the Barrio de Santa Cruz

WALKING TOURS VIA tour bus

Sightseeing buses face a severe limitation in Sevilla, since many of the city's medieval streets can't accommodate large vehicles. To compensate, **City Sightseeing** (the red bus) offers guided walking tours of Parque María Luisa and the barrios of Santa Cruz, Macarena, and Triana to everyone who buys a bus ticket. The bus makes a circuit on main streets, so it does touch bases with the cathedral, the Alcázar, Torre del Oro, the University of Sevilla, and Isla Mágica on Isla de Cartuja. It can be useful if your time is limited. A free ticket for the Torre de los Perdigones overlook (see below) is one of the discounts included. The buses run every 20 to 30 minutes and cost 17€ for adults and 7€ for children for unlimited use in a 24-hour period. To purchase tickets ahead, visit www.citysightseeing.com.

spreading north from them and Parque María Luisa spreading south. Due west of the cathedral, heading toward the river, is Arenal, the former ship-building district now dominated by the bullring and its adjacent concert hall. The old commercial district expands north of Plaza Nueva and Plaza Santiago. Shopping is anchored by Calles Sierpes and Cuna as they reach north to Plaza de Encarnación. The neighborhood north of Encarnación is called Macarena after the basilica, and stretches to the northern limit of the old city at the remains of the Moorish walls.

West of Sevilla's old city and across the river, the Barrio de Triana is the old fishermen's and Gypsy quarter, famed for its bullfighters, flamenco musicians, and ceramics in the North African tradition. The large Isla de Cartuja, north of Triana in the river, was the site of Expo '92 and now holds some museums, performance centers, and an amusement park.

Alcázar ★★★ PALACE Technically the oldest European royal residence still in use (the king and queen stay here when they're in Sevilla), this complex of palaces and fortifications dates from the Almohad rule of Sevilla. It was, however, almost entirely rebuilt after the 1248 reconquest of Sevilla. The older, more austere building is the **Palacio Gótico** ★, built by Alfonso X ("the Wise") in the 13th century. Carlos V modified the Great Hall and the Sala de Fiestas to celebrate his 1526 wedding to his Habsburg cousin (an unfortunate union that triggered the genetic problems of the dynasty). The far more beautiful and much larger **Palacio Mudéjar** ★★★ was built in the 14th century by Pedro I ("the Cruel"), likely employing some of the same artisans who worked on the Alhambra in Granada. It's a tour de force of carved plaster and stone, delicate calligraphic friezes, carved wooden ceilings, and splendid decorative tiles. From the Dolls' Court to the Maidens' Court through the domed Ambassadors' Room, it contains some of the finest work of Sevillano artisans. Fernando and Isabel, who at one time lived in the Alcázar, welcomed Columbus here on his return from America. On the top floor, the Oratory of the Catholic Monarchs has a fine altar in polychrome tiles made by Pisano in 1504. The well-kept **gardens** ★ are alone worth the visit. Plan to spend about 1½ hours here.

Plaza del Triunfo s/n. ✆ **95-450-23-23.** www.patronato-alcazar sevilla.es. Admission 9.50€ adults, 2.50€ seniors and students, free under age 17. Oct–Mar daily 9:30am–5pm; Apr–Sept daily 9:30am–7pm. Bus: T1.

Archivo General de Indias ★ LIBRARY   The Spanish crown administered its overseas empire from Sevilla, which also served as the landing port for gold and silver bullion. Such an enterprise generated a lot of paperwork, which was eventually filed away in this building. It is a mother lode of documents, enough of which are shown in rotating exhibitions to make for a fascinating visit. The building was designed by Felipe II's favorite architect, Juan de Herrera, as the Lonja (Stock Exchange). In the 17th century, it was head-quarters for the Academy of Sevilla, founded in part by the great Spanish artist Murillo. In 1785, during the reign of Carlos III, the building was turned over for use as a general records office for the Indies. Today's Archivo General de Indias contains some 4 million documents, including letters between patron queen Isabel and explorer Columbus. These very rare documents are locked in air-conditioned storage to keep them from disintegrating. On display in glass cases are fascinating documents in which the dreams of the early explorers come alive.

Av. de la Constitución. ✆ **95-450-05-28.** www.mcu.es. Free admission. Mon–Sat 9:30am–4:45pm; Sun 10am–1:45pm. Bus: T1.

Barrio de La Macarena ★ NEIGHBORHOOD The district around the **Basilica de La Macarena** ★ (Calle Bécquer, 1; ✆ **95-490-18-00**) is one of the most densely residential parts of the old city. To see the area at its best, spend a Saturday afternoon watching wedding parties come and go at the basilica. Men in traditional suits or tuxedos escort women resplendent in elegant shawls and flamenco-influenced designer dresses. When the happy couple rides off in their limousine, the Sevillanos pack into a bar across the street—and another wedding party floods into the church. You can also visit the church daily 9am to 2pm and 5 to 9pm. The 17th-century image of the **Virgen de Mararena** is one of the most venerated in the Holy Week processions. Church treasures are displayed in a separate **exposition room ★**, open the same hours. Admission with audioguide is 6€ adults, 4€ seniors and ages 16 and under.

Closer to the river than the basilica, the **Torre de los Perdigones ★** (Calle Resolana, 41; ℂ **95-490-93-53;** www.torredelosperdigones.com) is an 1890 industrial tower that has been converted into a scenic overlook with a camera obscura inside to project images of the city on the wall of a darkened room. It is open Monday to Thursday noon to 7pm, Friday to Sunday 11:30am to midnight. Admission is 4€ adults, 2.50€ ages 5 to 12.

Barrio de Santa Cruz ★★★ NEIGHBORHOOD
What was once a ghetto for Spanish Jews—who were forcibly expelled from Spain in 1492—is today one of Sevilla's most colorful districts. Near the old walls of the Alcázar, winding medieval streets with names like Vida (Life) and Muerte (Death) open onto pocket-size plazas. Part of the quintessential experience of visiting Sevilla is getting lost in the Barrio de Santa Cruz, only to stumble into a plaza where a waiter will offer you a seat and a drink. Flower-filled balconies with draping bougainvillea and potted geraniums jut over this labyrinth, shading you from the ferocious Andalucían sun. In the evening it's common to see Sevillanos sitting in the patios sipping wine under the glow of lanterns. To enter the Barrio de Santa Cruz, turn right after leaving the Patio de Banderas exit of the Alcázar. Turn right again at Plaza de la Alianza, going down Calle Rodrigo

Caro to Plaza de Doña Elvira. "Santa Crus" is also loosely applied to the dense streets of the Judería that lie just west of the main portion of Santa Cruz.

Barrio de Triana ★★ NEIGHBORHOOD Across the Guadalquivir from the city center, Triana is Sevilla with an edge. The working-class neighborhood is the traditional quarter of fishermen and *gitanos,* or Gypsies, and the birthplace of many famous bullfighters memorialized on street corners by commemorative plaques. This is also the neighborhood of *alfarerías,* makers of the traditional decorative tiles for which Sevilla is world famous. The tile companies are concentrated on Calle San Jorge and surrounding streets; most have sales rooms open to the public. Ceramics are very old in Triana—legend says that the neighborhood patrons,

The mosaic interior of Sevilla's Alcázar fortress.

3rd-century martyrs Santa Justa and Santa Rufina, were Triana potters.

The riverfront at the foot of Puente Isabel II is called the Puerto de Triana, and it is filled with small *tabernas* and *marisquerías* (shellfish restaurants) that set up outdoor tables during warm weather. This is the best area to head for early evening tapas as well as casual late-night flamenco (p. 38). Farther east along the river, approaching Puente San Telmo, Triana loses its rough edges and gives way to a number of handsome riverfront restaurants.

The historic public market, the **Mercado de Triana ★★**, is located at the end of Puente Isabel II. Redeveloped in 2012 to 2013, it has become a lively attraction in its own right, with a number of excellent tapas bars that serve food and drink well after the food stalls have closed. There is even a small theater in the market, which sometimes has lunchtime flamenco performances. The market sits directly next to the historic Moorish fortress known as the **Castillo de San Jorge ★**. There's no charge to visit San Jorge, which has archaeological exhibits showing its Almohad origins and an exhibition about the Spanish Inquisition, which was based here 1481 to 1785. Don't expect thumbscrews and instruments of torture—the exhibits delve sensitively into the causes (and practical political uses) of intolerance and persecution. San Jorge is open Monday to Friday 9am to 2pm, Saturday and Sunday 10am to 2pm.

Casa de Pilatos ★ HISTORIC HOUSE   This 16th-century Andalucían palace of the dukes of Medinaceli recaptures the splendor of the past, casually combining Gothic, Mudéjar, and Plateresque styles in its courtyards, fountains, and salons. Legend says that

Courtyard statue at Casa de Pilatos.

the house is a reproduction of Pilate's House in Jerusalem, but the distinctly Sevillano character of the architecture argues otherwise. The house has exhibits, supplemented by an audioguide, on both the ground floor and the first floor, used until recently by the family. The interior includes a collection of paintings by Carreño, Pantoja de la Cruz, Sebastiano del Piombo, Lucas Jordán, Batalloli, Pacheco, and Goya, as well as some atmospheric if not terribly accomplished Greek and Roman statuary. The lush gardens, however, are the highlight and are worth the entrance fee. The cascading magenta bougainvillea at the entrance is an iconic image of great wealth in a desert climate like Sevilla's. The palace is about a 7-minute walk northeast of the cathedral on the northern edge of Barrio de Santa Cruz, in a warren of labyrinthine streets.

Plaza Pilatos 1. © **95-422-52-98.** Entire house 8€; ground floor, patio, and gardens 5€. Apr–Oct daily 9am–7pm; Nov–Mar daily 9am–6pm.

Catedral de Sevilla and La Giralda ★★ CATHE-DRAL The largest Gothic building in the world and the third-largest church in Europe, after St. Peter's in Rome and St. Paul's in London, the Catedral de Sevilla was designed by builders with a stated goal—that "those who come after us will take us for madmen." Construction began in the late 1400s on the site of the Almohad mosque and took centuries to complete. Just inside one portal, the tomb of Columbus is held by four carved pall-bearers.

A detail from the altar at Catedral de Sevilla.

Works of art abound here, many of them architectural, such as the 15th-century stained-glass windows, the iron screens (*rejas*) closing off the chapels, the elaborate 15th-century choir stalls, and the Gothic reredos above the main altar. On the feasts of Corpus Christi and the Immaculate Conception (and on the 3rd day of Feria), six boys (*Los Seises*) from the choir perform a ceremonial dance on the altar dressed in Renaissance plumed hats and wielding castanets. The treasury has works by Goya, Murillo, and Zurbarán, as well as a display of skulls (*sic transit gloria mundi*). You might spot young women praying before the gigantic Murillo painting of the *Vision de San Antonio*. They're asking St. Anthony, patron of the lovelorn, to send them a husband. After touring the dark interior, you emerge into the sunlight of the Patio de Naranjas (Orange Trees), with its fresh citrus scents and chirping birds.

La Giralda, the bell tower of the cathedral, is the city's most emblematic monument. Erected as a minaret in the 12th century, it has seen later additions, such as 16th-century bells. Those who climb to the

ROLLING ON THE river

Spanish galleons may no longer sail up the Río Guadalquivír laden with gold, but the river remains one of the great assets of Sevilla. Sightseeing cruises from **Cruceros Torre del Oro** depart from the embankment just below the Torre del Oro at Paseo Muelle Marqués del Contadero. The cruise gives the best possible perspective on Sevilla's bridges, including the four that were constructed from the city to the Isla de Cartuja for Expo '92. The most dramatic of the group is the counter-balanced cable-stay Puente Alamillo designed by Santiago Calatrava. The form of the bridge has been variously compared to the prow of a ship or the shape of a harp. Either way, it is a lyrical image on the skyline. April to October, cruises depart every 30 minutes from 10am to 8pm; November to March they depart every half-hour 11am to 7pm. For information, call ✆ **95-456-16-92,** or visit www.cruceros torredeloro.com. The cruise costs 15€ for adults; children under 12 are free.

top ascend on a ramp constructed so that the muezzin could ride up on horseback. Those who make it up get a dazzling view of Sevilla. Entrance is through the cathedral.

Av. de la Constitución s/n. ✆ **95-421-49-71.** www.catedralde sevilla.es. Cathedral and tower 8€ adults, 3€ students 25 and under, free for children 14 and under. Sept–June Mon 11am–3:30pm, Tue–Sat 11am–5pm, Sun 2:30–6pm; July–Aug Mon 9:30am–3:30pm, Tue–Sat 9:30am–4:30pm, Sun 2:30-6:30pm. Bus: T1.

Metropol Parasol ★★ LANDMARK   Finally completed in 2011, this sprawling wooden structure overshadows the Plaza de la Encarnación with six parasols in mushroom shapes. Locals simply call it "Las Setas"

(Spanish for "mushrooms") and you have to see it to believe it. The plaza had been the site of a public market for more than a century. When excavations began to build a new one, Roman and Moorish ruins were found underground, delaying the process for years. Now the underground portion is the Antiquarium, a well-interpreted archaeological site, and the sculptural Las Setas, designed by German architect Jürgen Mayer-Hermann, towers above a new upscale public market that features tapas bars, delis and food stalls. Upper levels of Las Setas include an observation deck and restaurant.

Plaza de la Encarnación, s/n. ✆ **60-663-52-14.** www.setasde sevilla.com. Viewing level 3€; Antiquarium 2.10€. Market Mon–Sat 8am–3pm. Antiquarium Tues–Sat 10am–8pm, Sun 10am–2pm. Viewing level Sun–Thurs 10:30am–11:45pm, Fri–Sat 10:30am–12:45am. Bus: 27, 32, A2.

Museo de Bellas Artes de Sevilla ★★ MUSEUM

The convent building that houses this extensive collection of Spanish art nearly upstages the paintings inside. Built in 1594 for the order of the Merced Calzada de la Asunción, it benefited from Sevilla's golden age of painting and ceramics (the courtyard tiles are enthralling). Inside the galleries are the greatest works of Bartolomé Esteban Murillo, including a gigantic image of the Immaculate Conception originally painted for the Convento de San Francisco. Other highlights include works by Sevilla-born Juan Valdés Leal, and Francisco de Zurbarán.

Plaza del Museo 9. ✆ **95-478-65-00.** www.museosdeandalucia. es. Admission 1.50€, free to E.U. residents and students. Mid-Sept–May Tues–Sat 10am–8:30pm, Sun 10am–5pm; June–mid-Sept Tues–Sat 9am-3:30pm; Sun 10am–5pm. Bus: C5.

Museo del Baile Flamenco ★★ MUSEUM

It has been said that there are no schools to create flamenco dancers, just as there are none to create poets. Cristina Hoyos, the founder of this museum, drew instead on her depth of feeling to become one of the most celebrated flamenco dancers of the late 20th century. The impressionistic museum is relatively short on signage and long on film clips and videos that immerse the viewer in the art of the dance. One of the most engrossing exhibits features short videos that demonstrate the seven representative styles (*palos*) of flamenco from the solea to the tangos. In an opening video, Hoyos advises viewers to follow their emotions. It's not necessary to understand flamenco, she asserts. It must be felt. See for yourself at a nightly show (see below).

Calle Manuel Rojas Marcos, 3. © **95-434-03-11**. www.museo flamenco.com. Admission 10€ adults, 8€ students and seniors, 6€ children. Daily 10am–7pm. Bus: C5.

Museo Palacio de la Condesa de Lebrija ★ HISTORIC HOUSE   Nominally a museum of architecture and interior decoration, this historic house is a portrait of the Countess of Lebrija, who owned the 16th-century palace from 1901 until 1914. She installed a number of ancient mosaics (some Roman, some Moorish) and decorated with a surprisingly harmonious collection of Roman, Greek, and Persian statues as well as Louis XVI furniture to go with her 2nd- and 3rd-century b.c. Roman mosaic floors.

Calle Cuna, 8. © **95-422-78-02**. www.palaciodelebrija.com. Admission 8€ both floors, 5€ ground floor. Sept–June Mon–Fri 1:30am–7:30pm, Sat 10am–2pm and 4–8pm, Sun 10am–2pm; July Mon–Fri 9am–3pm, Sat 10am–2pm; Aug Mon–Fri 10am–3pm, Sat 10am–2pm. Bus: 27, 32, A2.

Parque María Luisa ★ PARK   This park, dedicated to María Luisa, sister of Isabel II, was once the grounds of the **Palacio de San Telmo.** The palace, whose baroque facade is visible behind the deluxe Alfonso XIII Hotel, today houses a seminary. In 1929, Sevilla hosted the Exposición Iberoamericana, and many Latin-American countries erected showcase buildings and pavilions in and around the park. Many pavillions still stand, serving as foreign consulates or university buildings. The park is one of the most tranquil areas in the city and attracts Sevillanos who want to row boats on its ponds, walk along flower-bordered paths, jog, or bicycle. The most romantic (if expensive) way to traverse the park is by horse and carriage.

Plaza de América ★ SQUARE This landmark square, abloom with flowers, shade trees, and exquisite fountains, represents city planning at its best. It houses a trio of pavilions left over from the 1929 Expo. The center holds government offices; on either side are minor museums worth visiting if you have time to spare.

The **Museo Arqueológico Provincial** ★ (© 95-478-64-74) contains many artifacts from prehistoric times and the days of the Romans, Visigoths, and Moors. It's open September to June Tuesday to Saturday 10am to 8:30pm, and Sunday 9am to 2:30pm; in July it's open Monday to Friday 9am to 3pm, Saturday 10am to 2pm; in August it's open Monday to Friday 10am to 3pm and Saturday 10am to 2pm. Admission is 1.50€ for adults and free for E.U. residents and students. Buses 30, 31, and 34 stop there. Nearby is the **Museo de Artes y Costumbres Populares** ★ (© 95-471-23-91; www.museosdeandalucia.es). In a Mudéjar pavilion opposite the Museo Arqueológico, this is Sevilla's folklore museum. The ground floor displays artifacts of traditional occupations, including a forge, a baker's oven, a wine press, and a tanner's shop. The ceramics collection on this floor is first-rate. The upstairs is devoted to fashion and costumes, including court dress of the 19th century and embroideries from the factories of Sevilla. It's open September to June Tuesday to Saturday 9am to 8:30pm, and Sunday 9am to 2:30pm; July to August Tuesday to Saturday 9am to 3:30pm, Sunday 10am to 5pm. Admission is 1.50€ for adults, free to E.U. residents and students.

Plaza de España ★ SQUARE   The major building left over from the Exposición Iberoamericana at the Parque María Luisa is the crescent-shaped Renaissance-style structure set on this landmark square. Architect Aníbal González not only designed but supervised construction of the immense structure. You can rent rowboats for excursions on the canal, or you can walk across bridges spanning it. Set into a curved wall are alcoves focusing on the characteristics of Spain's 50 provinces, as depicted in tile murals.

Torre del Oro ★ MUSEUM   The Almohad rulers of Sevilla erected this tower and another just like it across the river in 1220 as a defensive mechanism. A stout chain linked the two, preventing ships from moving in and out of the port without authorization. The system proved fruitless when a Castillian

Torre del Oro.

admiral broke the chain during the 1248 siege. The complementary tower vanished centuries ago, but the Torre del Oro has stood for nearly 9 centuries, serving at various times as administrative offices and a warehouse. Its name derives from the unusual yellow-tinged plaster made of mortar, lime, and straw. These days it serves as the Museo Marítimo and recounts the history of port from its Almohad era to its shipping heyday of the 16th and 17th centuries.

Paseo de Cristóbal Colón, s/n. © **95-422-24-19.** Admission 3€ adults, 1.50€ seniors and students; free Mon. Mon–Fri 9:30am–6:45pm; Sat–Sun 10:30am–6:45pm. Bus: 3, 40, 41, C4, C5. Metro Linea 1: Puerta de Jerez.

Real Plaza de Toros ★ LANDMARK

The Real Maestranza de Caballería de Sevilla began construction of this slightly oval bullring in 1761 to replace earlier wooden rings. It was completed in stages over the following 120 years and is one of the oldest and loveliest rings in the country. Guided tours begin in the stands, which seat 12,000 people. Although visitors cannot step onto the orange earth of the ring, they

A matador faces down a bull at Real Maestranza de Caballería de Sevilla.

can survey the five gates that help orchestrate the *corrida*, including the gates where matadors and bulls enter the ring, the gate where dead bulls are carried out by three mules, and the gate where matadors exit in triumph if they receive the highest honors from the officials. The paintings and sculptures in the museum help trace the history of the spectacle from an aristocratic demonstration of bravery to a more populist sport in which talented bullfighters can achieve the fame of nobility. A number of bullfighters' costumes are on display, along with the red capes (*muletas*) that the bullfighter uses to attract the bull. Bulls, by the way, are colorblind; they respond to the motion, not the traditional color.

Paseo Colón, 12. © **95-421-03-15.** www.realmaestranza.com. Admission 7€ adults, 4€ seniors and students. Open Nov–Apr daily 9:30am–7pm, May and Oct daily 9:30am–8pm, June–Sept daily 9:30am–11pm. Bus: 3, 40, 41, C4, C5.

Shopping

Calle Sierpes is the main pedestrian shopping promenade in Sevilla. Shops of note include **Artesanía Textil,** Calle Sierpes, 70 (© **95-456-28-40;** www.artesania-textil.com), which sells investment-quality hand-embroidered silk shawls. The clerks are equally helpful if you're interested in a more modestly priced piece that will still look fabulous back home. **Sombrería Maquedano,** Calle Sierpes, 40 (© **95-456-47-71**), sells beautiful men's felt hats ranging from classic Borsalinos to the flatter, wide-brimmed caballero's hat.

To see the evolution of Sevillana style, stroll Calle Cuna, which runs parallel to Sierpes. The shop windows are a fashion show of flamenco wear and flamenco-inspired contemporary fashion. But it's not all ruffles and dangly earrings. Founded in 1892, **El**

Caballo, Calle Adriano, 16 (✆ **95-421-81-27**), near the bullring, sells traditional saddlery, riding equipment, and fashion accessories, including beautiful leather purses and belts.

It's almost impossible to leave Sevilla without buying a piece of pottery. Near the cathedral, **El Azulejo,** Calle Mateos Gago, 10 (✆ **95-422-00-85**), has fine ceramic pieces in a wide range of prices as well as handpainted fans. In Santa Cruz, **Las Moradas Artesanía Andalusí,** Calle Rodrigo Caro, 20 (✆ **95-456-39-17**), has large painted tiles of medieval scenes as well as one of the best selections of gift items (from leatherwork and scarves to hair combs and earrings made of plastic that mimics tortoise shell). It is worth a visit to Triana to see the tile-encrusted facade of **Cerámica Santa Ana,** Calle San Jorge, 31, (✆ **95-433-39-90**). The factory and showroom, which opened in 1870, has a broad selection of painted tiles, pots, tableware, and decorative items in the *azulejo* tradition. A serving bowl for olives with a separate compartment for pits makes an authentic Spanish souvenir. Right down the street in **Cerámica Rocio-Triana,** Calle Antillano Campos, 8 (✆ **95-434-06-50**), a husband and wife team create more unusual pieces.

If you want a bullfight poster, skip the tourist shops that offer to print your name on a generic poster and visit the shop at the Plaza de Toros, where artist-designed posters from previous seasons are for sale.

Sevilla for Children

Children delight at feeding cracked corn to the white pigeons in **Plaza de América** (p. 33), and you'll definitely want a photo as the birds flock to their outstretched hands. They'll also get a kick out of climbing the series of ramps to the bell tower of **La Giralda**

(p. 28) and taking a cruise on the Río Guadalquivír (p. 30). Across the river at Isla de Cartuja, the site of Expo '92, interactive educational displays at the **Pabellón de la Navegación,** Camino de los Descubrimientos (© 95-404-31-11), capture the sense of adventure of the early navigators whose discoveries helped make Spain rich and powerful. Many of the accurate ship models on display were made for the Expo. A highlight of the visit is the 50m (164-ft.) Torre Mirador, which offers panoramic views of the city. The Pavilion of Navigation is open from November to April Tuesday to Saturday 10am to 7:30pm; Sunday 10am to 3pm. In May, June, September, and October it is open Tuesday to Saturday 11am to 8:30pm; Sunday 11am to 3pm. In July and August hours are Tuesday to Sunday 10am to 3pm.

Also on the site of Expo '92, the amusement park **Isla Mágica,** Rotonda Isla Mágica (© 90-216-17-16; www.islamagica.es), captures the fun side of the Expo with rides, entertainment and a waterpark that opened in 2014. Isla Mágica is open daily 11am to 11pm (until midnight on Sat) in July and August with more limited hours April to June and September to early November. Adult admission is 22€ for a full day and 16€ for a half-day. Children and senior citizens are 15€ for a whole day and 10€ for a half-day.

Nightlife
FLAMENCO
If you only have one night in Sevilla, you should go to flamenco. The city is a cradle of the art form, and has the busiest performance schedule in the country outside Madrid. There are three formats to choose among.

Two educational centers offer very pure flamenco in a style intended to be as educational as it is entertaining.

The **Museo del Baile Flamenco,** Calle Manuel Rojas Marcos, 13 (© **95-434-03-11;** www.museoflamenco. com), offers dance-oriented performances in its courtyard daily at 7pm. Admission is 20€ for adults, 14€ seniors and students, and 12€ children. The **Casa de la Memoria de Al Andalus,** Calle Cuna, 6 (© **95-456-06-70;** www.casadelamemoria.es), has two shows per night in a small courtyard space, usually featuring a small troupe of a musician or two, a singer, and one or two dancers. The emphasis here is on early 20th-century styles that emphasize singing as well as dancing. Shows are at 7:30pm and 9pm. Admission is 16€ adults, 14€ students, and 10€ ages 6 to 11. Arrive early, and you can also tour the flamenco history exhibitions.

The flamenco nightclub spectacle, or *tablao,* of choreographed flamenco performances is an honored tradition in Sevilla. Most *tablaos* give you a drink with basic admission and try to sell you a dinner for an extra 20€ to 40€. The dinner is rarely worth the price, but it is convenient and you may get better seats. **El Patio Sevillano,** Paseo de Cristóbal Colón, 11 (© **95-421-41-20;** www.elpatiosevillano.com), has 90-minute shows twice nightly at 7pm and 9:30pm. Admission is 37€. **El Arenal,** Calle Rodó, 7 (© **95-421-64-92;** www.tablaoelarenal.com), also has two nightly shows at 8pm and 10pm. Admission is 37€. At **Los Gallos,** Plaza de Santa Cruz, 11 (© **95-421-69-81;** www. tablaolosgallos.com), the twice-nightly, 2-hour shows begin at 8pm and 10:30pm. Admission is 35€ adults, 20€ children under 8.

Finally, there is the flamenco bar scene, where you may or may not encounter someone playing and/or dancing, but at least you don't have to sit politely in folding chairs. Three of the best are in Triana: **El Rejoneo,** Calle Betis, 31B; the dance club **Lo Nuestro** next door at Calle Betis, 31A on Tuesdays and Thursdays; and **T de Triana,** Calle Betis, 20. They all open between 11pm and midnight and stay open until dawn.

DRINKS & TAPAS

Most Spaniards consider an evening of snacking and drinking to be the definition of a good time. An excellent tapas scene fills **Calle Joaquín Guichot,** a street parallel with the south side of Plaza Nueva, and spills out westward on **Calle Zaragoza.** Another very popular spot for drinks and tapas is the **Gastrosol,** the bar at Las Setas (Metropol Parasol) in Plaza de Encarnación. As the night advances on Wednesdays through Saturdays, prowl the **Alameda de Hercules** for the best in dance clubs and cocktail bars, which don't open before 10 or 11pm. Most are at least gay-friendly, and those that are overtly gay also welcome a straight crowd. A couple of the best bets are **Bar 1987,** Alameda de Hercules, 93, where shoulder pads, mullets, and Euro disco prove that the Eighties never died. **Bar El Barón Rampante,** Calle Arias Montano, 3, is one of the most popular spots.

PERFORMING ARTS

Though often the setting for operas, Sevilla didn't get its own opera house until the 1990s. The **Teatro de la Maestranza,** Paseo de Colón, 22 (© **95-422-33-44;** www.teatromaestranza.com), quickly became one of the world's premier venues for opera. The season focuses on works inspired by the city, including Verdí's *La Forza del Destino* and Mozart's *Marriage of Figaro,* although jazz, classical music, and even Spanish *zarzuelas* (operettas) are also performed here. The opera house may be visited only during performances. Tickets (which vary in price, depending on the event) can be purchased daily from 10am to 2pm and 5:30 to 8:30pm at the box office in front of the theater.

Side Trips

CARMONA ★

An easy hour-long bus trip from the main terminal in Sevilla, Carmona is an ancient city that dates from Neolithic times and contains important Roman ruins. Thirty-four kilometers (21 miles) east of Sevilla, it grew in power and prestige under the Moors, establishing ties with Castilla in 1252.

Surrounded by fortified walls, Carmona has three Moorish fortresses—one a *parador,* and the other two the Alcázar de la Puerta de Córdoba and the Alcázar de la Puerta de Sevilla. The most impressive attraction is **Puerta de Sevilla,** with its double Moorish arch opposite Iglesia de San Pedro. Note, too, **Puerta de Córdoba,** on Calle Santa María de Gracia, which was attached to the ancient Roman walls in the 17th century.

The town itself is a national landmark, filled with narrow streets, whitewashed walls, and Renaissance mansions. The most important square, **Plaza San Fernando,** is lined with elegant 17th-century houses. The most important church is dedicated to Santa María and stands on Calle Martín López. You enter a Moorish patio before exploring the interior and its 15th-century white vaulting.

In the area known as Jorge Bonsor (named for the original discoverer of the ruins) is a **Roman amphitheater** as well as a **Roman necropolis** containing the remains of 1,000 families who lived in and around Carmona 2,000 years ago. Of the two important tombs, the Elephant Vault consists of three dining rooms and a kitchen. The other, the Servilia Tomb, is the size of a nobleman's villa. The **Museo de la Ciudad** (© 95-423-24-01; www.museociudad.carmona.org; 3€ adults, free for students and children) displays artifacts discovered at the site. At press time it was closed for renovations (check website for info).

If you're driving to Carmona, exit from Sevilla's eastern periphery onto the N-V superhighway, follow the signs to the airport, and then proceed to Carmona on the road to Madrid. The Carmona turnoff is clearly marked.

To stay overnight, try the elegant **Casa de Carmona ★★**, Plaza de Lasso 1, (© 95-419-10-00; www.casadecarmona.com). This 16th-century private home turned luxury hotel retains the marble columns, imposing masonry, and graceful proportions of the original structure. Each of the 33 units is opulently furnished in a Roman, Moorish, or Renaissance theme. Rates are 68€ to 158€ double, 148€ to 218€ junior suite.

ITÁLICA ★

Lovers of Roman history shouldn't miss Itálica (© 95-562-22-66), the ruins of an ancient city northwest of Sevilla on the major road to Lisbon.

After the battle of Ilipa, Publius Cornelius Scipio Africanus founded Itálica in 206 B.C. Two of the most famous Roman emperors, Trajan and Hadrian, were born here. Indeed, master builder Hadrian was to have a major influence on his hometown. During his reign, the **amphitheater,** the ruins of which can be seen today, was among the largest in the Roman Empire. Lead pipes that carried water from the Río Guadalquivír still remain. A small **museum** displays some of the Roman statuary found here, although the finest pieces have been shipped to Sevilla. Many mosaics, depicting beasts, gods, and birds, are on exhibit, and others are constantly being discovered. The ruins, including a Roman theater, can be explored for 1.50€ (free to E.U. residents). The site is open April to May and the second half of September Tuesday to Saturday 9am to 8pm and Sunday 9am to 3pm. From June to mid-September, it's open Tuesday to Saturday 9am to 3:30pm and Sunday 10am to 5pm. From mid-September to March, it's open Tuesday to Saturday 9am to 6:30pm and Sunday 10am to 4pm.

If you're driving, exit from the northwest periphery of Sevilla, and follow the signs for Highway E-803 in the direction of Zafra and Lisbon. A bus marked M-172 goes to Itália, and departures are from Sevilla's Estación de Autobuses at Plaza de Armas. Buses depart every hour for the 30-minute trip.

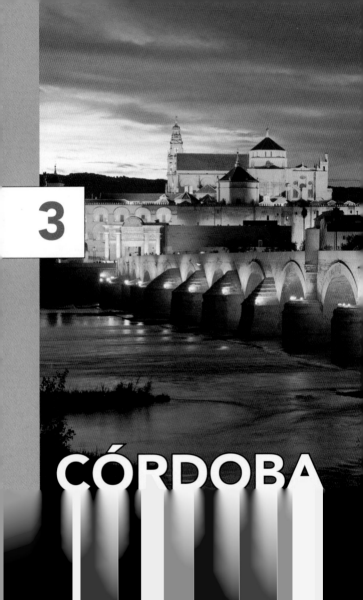

3

CÓRDOBA

To visit Córdoba is to glimpse what might have been. A millennium ago, Muslims, Christians, and Jews lived and worked together to create western Europe's greatest city—a cosmopolitan center of poetry, art, music, philosophy, cutting-edge science and medicine, and far-ranging scholarship. Until the late 11th century, Córdoba was the capital of western Islam. La Mezquita, the largest medieval mosque in Europe, remains its star attraction. The streets and whitewashed buildings of Andalucía's most intact Moorish city still endure, and visiting Córdoba is ultimately less about monuments and more about getting lost in the maze of cobbled streets that bore witness to an ancient, harmonious world.

You can hit the highlights in a long day, but Córdoba deserves the attention that comes from staying overnight, if only to experience the timeless Judería just after dawn, when you can hear the echoing step of every foot in the narrow streets. There are other advantages to staying the night. Every morning from 8:30 to 9:20am (except Sun), you can visit La Mezquita in

PREVIOUS PAGE: **The Old Cathedral (Mezquita) of Cordoba at night**

CÓRDOBA'S gastromarket IS A HIT

A short distance northwest of the Judería, a transplanted fair pavilion in the Jardines de Victoria was transformed in May 2013 into the first gastronomic market in Andalucía, **Mercado Victoria,** Paseo de la Victoria, s/n (www.mercado victoria.com). The 30 food stalls cover all the bases of a conventional fresh-food market—fish, meat, produce, baked goods, and beverages—but most also offer food for immediate consumption on premise. There's also a workshop kitchen for classes and demonstrations. By early evening, the entire glassed-in pavilion is jammed with people eating and drinking, making it one of the most lively tapas scenes in town.

silence to get a sense of its truly meditative power (no admission is charged). Moreover, Artencordoba (www.artencordoba.com) offers 2-hour guided night tours of the city.

Essentials

GETTING THERE   Córdoba is a crossroads for high-speed rail between Madrid and Sevilla, Madrid and Málaga, and Málaga and Sevilla, as well as for *media distancia* (MD) trains between Jaen and Sevilla. About 30 **high-speed trains** per day arrive from Madrid, taking about 2 hours and costing 62€ each way. Many use the high-speed link for day trips from Sevilla. The AVE costs 30€, while AVANT trains (20€) and MD trains (13€) take only minutes longer. To visit from the Costa del Sol, take one of the 19 trains per day from Málaga, all take about an hour and cost 41€ for AVE and 27€ for AVANT.

The main train station is north of the old city at Glorieta de las Tres Culturas, off Avenida de América. Bus 3 runs between the rail station and the historic core. Otherwise, it is about a 15-minute walk south on Avenida de Cervantes or Avenida del Gran Capitán. For rail information, call © **90-242-22-42;** for AVE information, call © **90-242-22-42.** The RENFE advance-ticket office in Córdoba is at Ronda de los Tejares 10 (© **95-747-58-84;** www.renfe.com).

Alsa (© **95-740-40-40;** www.alsa.es) provides **bus** service to Córdoba to the station behind the train depot on Glorieta de las Tres Culturas. The most popular routes are between Córdoba and Sevilla, with seven buses per day. The trip takes 2 hours and costs 12€ one-way. Between Granada and Córdoba eight to nine buses per day make the 3-hour run; the cost is 13€ for a one-way ticket.

VISITOR INFORMATION The **tourist office,** Calle Torrijos, 10 (© **95-735-51-79;** www.andalucia.org), is open Monday to Friday 9am to 6:30pm, Saturday and Sunday 9:30am to 3pm.

Where to Stay

At the peak of its summer season, Córdoba has too few hotels to meet the demand, so reserve as far in advance as possible.

EXPENSIVE

Las Casas de la Judería ★★ This romantic hotel sits in the heart of the Judería. Once you step through the heavy wooden door you'll feel as if you're in another world. Created from adjacent 17th- and 18th-century city palaces, the guest rooms feature beds with elaborate headboards and rich bedding. Rooms vary in size and some are quite small. But the public areas are the real joy of the property, and you can experience the Córdoban lifestyle of outdoor living as you enjoy the patios, fountain, and shaded arcades.

Calle Tomás Conde, 10. ☏ **95-720-20-95**. www.casasypalacios. com. 64 rooms. 109€–245€ double; 225€–383€ jr. suites. Parking 19€. Bus: 2, 3, 5, 6. **Amenities:** Restaurant; bar; pool; free Wi-Fi.

MODERATE

NH Amistad Córdoba ★★　The Amistad is literally part of the city—a portion of its back wall is built right into the walls of Córdoba's old city. In the often familiar pattern of historic lodgings, architects combined two 18th-century mansions to make a gracious hotel, and later added another building across the Plaza de Maimónides for suites. In contrast with the historic Mudéjar-style patio at the heart of the property, the generally spacious rooms are decorated in clean-lined modern style of dark woods and richly colored fabrics.

Plaza de Maimónides, 3. ☏ **95-742-03-35.** www.nh-hoteles. com. 108 units. 75€–197€ double; 115€–225 jr. suite. Parking 20€. Bus: 2, 3, 5, or 6. **Amenities:** Restaurant; bar; pool; free Wi-Fi.

INEXPENSIVE

Hotel Marisa ★　Literally across the street from La Mezquita, the Marisa closed for several months at the end of 2013 to paint and refresh all the rooms and improve the heating and air-conditioning. Alas, they could not make the rooms any larger, but what the rooms may lack in dimensions, the hotel makes up for with friendly staff and an excellent location. If you are a light sleeper, ask for a room that looks out on the interior patio. Two rooms at the front of the hotel have views of La Mezquita. All are modestly furnished and well-maintained.

Calle Cardenal Herrero, 6. ✆ **95-747-31-42.** www.hotelmarisa. es. 38 units. 45€–125€ double. Parking 15€. Bus: 3 or 16. **Amenities:** Bar; free Wi-Fi.

Los Omeyas ★ Los Omeyas, in the Juderia, makes a good bargain-priced base for exploring—and for taking a break from the often crowded narrow streets. The simple front door doesn't really prepare you for the sight of the lovely arched patio at the heart of the building. Rooms are modest with dark wood furniture and light walls and fabrics. For city views, request a room on the top floor.

Calle Encarnación, 17, ✆ **95-749-22-67.** www.hotel-los omeyas.com. 39 units. 40€–80€ double. Parking 15€. Bus: 3 or 16. **Amenities:** Bar; free Wi-Fi.

Where to Eat

Córdoban cuisine probably draws more extensively on Arabic and North African cooking than anywhere else in Spain. Not only does it liberally mix sweet flavors into savory dishes, you'll find a lot of dried fruits and nuts and such spices as cumin, turmeric, and cinnamon. Lamb and kid are usually the meats of choice, although many menus feature beef, a side effect of the local bull-breeding industry. It wouldn't be Spain without a strong complement of pork and shellfish—dishes banned by Jewish and Muslim dietary laws.

MODERATE

Los Caballerizas de los Marqueses ★★ ANDALUCIAN   With dining areas in an outdoor patio and a covered dining room inside the hotel Las Casas de la Judería, this exquisite restaurant run by chef Oscar Hidalgo González offers perhaps the most refined

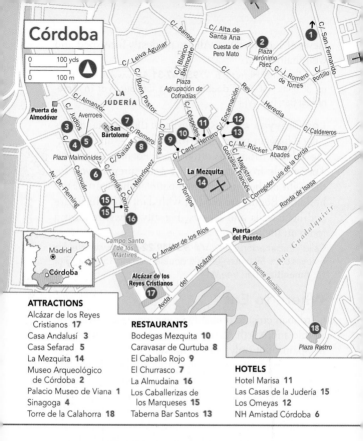

Córdoba

0   100 yds
0   100 m

LA JUDERÍA

Puerta de Almodóvar

La Mezquita 14

Puerta del Puente

Río Guadalquivir

Campo Santo de los Mártires

Alcázar de los Reyes Cristianos 17

Puente Romano

Plaza Rastro

Madrid

Córdoba

dining experience in town. Dishes draw extensively on traditional Córdoban cooking, but they're updated for lighter, more modern tastes. Fish specialties include oven-roasted sea bass with baby green beans and mint. Hidalgo serves roast suckling pig already deboned and topped with an amontillado sauce. The desserts (of which there are many) tend to feature fruit—except

the white chocolate mousse with rose-petal ice cream,
though it comes garnished with fresh berries.

Calle Tomás Conde, 10. © **95-720-20-95.** www.casasypalacios.
com. Main courses 15€–20€. Daily noon–4pm and 8–11pm.
Bus: 2, 3, 5, or 6.

La Almudaina ★★ ANDALUCIAN   Set into a
16th-century mansion in the old city walls near the
Alcázar, Almudaina affects a more international style
than most Córdoban restaurants, offering pork sirloin
with truffle sauce and finishing swordfish steak in a
brandy sauce with wild mushrooms. But the kitchen
also prepares some great regional classics. In fact, you
can taste six of them plus dessert on the tapas tasting
menu that includes *salmorejo* (tomato cream with ham
and grated egg), fried meatballs stuffed with mountain
ham, stewed oxtail, and fried eggplant with honey.

Plaza Campos de los Santos Mártires 1. © **95-747-43-42.** www.
restaurantealmudaina.com. Tapas tasting menu 27€; main
courses 12€–25€. Mon–Sat 12:30–4pm and 8:30pm–midnight;
Sun 12:30–4pm. Bus: 3 or 16.

El Caballo Rojo ★★ SPANISH   Across the street
from the Patio de las Naranjas, the Red Horse sits at
the end of a whitewashed passageway hung with pots of
blooming geraniums, begonias, and impatiens. The restaurant is as lovely as its entrance, spreading 300 seats
through two levels of dining rooms. The chef-owner is
something of a scholar of Córdoban foodways, which
makes for some interesting dishes adapted from Sephardic and Mozarabic traditions. Along with the classics
(beef sirloin, roast pork, baked fish), you'll find some
dishes here rarely served outside people's homes, such
as lamb sweetbreads or partridge stewed with kidney
beans. The house version of artichokes steamed in
Montilla wine won first prize in a national gastronomic

competition. Desserts are a big deal and many are made with egg yolks, almonds, dates, and other flavors of the Moorish tradition. You'll find them hard to resist when the dessert cart rolls by.

Calle Cardinal Herrero, 28. © **95-747-53-75.** www.elcaballo rojo.com. Main courses 14€–26€; fixed-price menu 26€. Daily 1–4:30pm and 8pm–midnight. Bus: 2.

El Churrasco ★ ANDALUCIAN   Arabic influences lend interesting flavors to the grilled meats at El Churrasco. Grilled pork sirloin, for example, is served with *salsas arabes,* a gravy seasoned with cumin and cinnamon. But El Churrasco is also a good place to sample the Andalucían standard, *rabo de toro,* or stewed oxtail, especially satisfying for those with hearty appetites. Several fish options are also available, ranging from red tuna tartare with trout eggs to turbot roasted with clams and shrimp.

Calle Romero, 16. © **95-729-08-19.** www.elchurrasco.com. Tapas 2€–11€; main courses 12€–26€; fixed-price menu 32€ (Mon–Fri). Sun–Thurs 1–4:30pm and 8:30–11:30pm; Fri–Sat 1–4pm and 8:30pm–midnight. Bus: 3.

INEXPENSIVE

Bodegas Mezquita ★★ ANDALUCIAN   Originally a deli and wine store, Bodegas Mezquita has expanded to become a full-blown bar and restaurant. The bar opens first; as more customers arrive, the waiters open other rooms until the whole place is packed. The wine list emphasizes bottles from Córdoba province but includes good choices from all over Spain. Most of the dishes are offered in a choice of sizes, making it easy to order tapas and taste several. Crisply fried slices of eggplant are served with honey, and the bodega offers a stew of the day. For a local specialty, try the Córdoban rice pot with stewed Iberian pork and mushrooms, or the Sephardic lamb stew with nuts and raisins and a side of couscous.

Calle Céspedes, 12. ℂ **95-749-00-04.** www.bodegasmezquita. com. Tapas 2.60€–4.50€; main dishes 6.50€–15€; tapas menu 13€; daily menu 15€. Daily noon–midnight. Bus: 2.

Caravasar de Qurtuba ★ ANDALUCIAN The sign for Lola Hotel still hangs outside (and there is one room available upstairs in this gorgeous central-courtyard building), but Lola Carmona Morales converted the ground level and first floor into a tearoom in 2013, making it a welcome respite from the hubbub of the Judería and the crush of the bars. You can get fruit drinks and coffees here, but the main point is to have a pot of freshly brewed tea and a plate of Arabic pastries.

Calle Romero, 3. ℂ **95-720-03-05.** Arabic pastries and tea 2€–4€. Sun 11–10, Tues–Thurs 11–11, Fri–Sat 11-midnight. Bus: 3, 12.

Taberna Bar Santos ★ ANDALUCIAN When Francisco Santos opened this tiny bar next to La Mezquita in 1966, he knew he needed something to set his place apart. That something became a massive *tortilla Española,* or potato omelet, that has been called the best in Spain. The creamy slices attract crowds of patrons who spill out into the street. Among the other tapas, we like the tuna topped with roasted red peppers and the bowl of *salmorejo* with slices of bread. This is a cash-only establishment.

Calle Magistral González Frances, 3. ℂ **95-748-89-75.** taberna barsantos.com. Tapas 2€–7€. Daily 10am–midnight. Bus: 2.

Exploring Córdoba

Among Córdoba's many sights is the **Puente Romano (Roman Bridge)** ★, dating from the time of Caesar Augustus and crossing the Guadalquivir River about a block south of the Mezquita. It's Roman in form only, as all 16 supporting arches have been replaced at one time or another in the last 2,000 years. Sculptor Bernabé Gómez del Río erected a statue of archangel San Rafael at the midpoint in 1651; it's a favorite spot for romantic poses.

Chances are, however, that you will spend most of your time in Córdoba within the medieval walled city with its narrow, winding streets. Buildings are so old and have so many layers of whitewash that few of them have a single sharp corner remaining. This area is known as the **Judería ★★★**, although it was, in fact, home to Christians, Jews, and Muslims alike for several hundred years. Most visitors enter the Judería from the streets around La Mezquita, but to get an idea of how the medieval gates looked, enter via the northwest entrance at the **Puerta de Almodóvar ★**.

There's no gate still standing where Calle Manriquez meets Calle Dr. Fleming, as 16th-century houses have taken its place. When construction workers began excavating here under the Plaza Campos de los Santos Mártires, they found the remains of the old Moorish

The Puente Romano, or Roman Bridge, in Córdoba.

A garden at the Alcázar de los Reyes Cristianos.

baths associated with the Alcázar, the **Baños del Alcázar Califal de Córdoba ★**. The interpretation is first rate. They are open Tuesday to Friday from 8:30am to 8:45pm, Saturday 8:30am to 4:30pm, and Sunday 8:30am to 2:30pm. Admission is 2.50€ for adults, 1.25€ for students, free under 14 years old, and free to all Tuesday to Friday 8:30 to 9:30am.

Alcázar de los Reyes Cristianos ★★ PALACE Commissioned in 1328 by Alfonso XI, the Alcázar of the Christian Kings is a fine example of military architecture. Fernando and Isabel governed Spain from this fortress on the river as they prepared to re-conquer Granada, the last Moorish stronghold in Spain. Columbus journeyed here to fill Isabel's ears with his plans for discovery. A statue commemorates Columbus's audience and the rulers' agreement to underwrite his exploratory voyage of 1492.

Two blocks west of La Mezquita, the Alcázar is notable for powerful walls and a trio of towers: the Tower of the Lions, the Tower of Allegiance, and the Tower of the River. While not as inspiring as La Mezquita, the Alcázar was the backdrop to a number of important historical events. The regional branch of the

Spanish Inquisition was based here from 1490 until 1821, and Franco later turned the fortress into a prison. But the troubled past is behind it now. Some of the larger halls display 3rd- and 4th-century A.D. Roman mosaics unearthed in Córdoba, while the formal 18th-century gardens hold ever-changing flower beds, long lines of sculpted cypresses, and fragrant orange trees.

There is a sound and light spectacle on Mondays, when the Alcázar is otherwise closed, and on Saturday afternoons from 4:30 to 8pm.

Calle Caballerizas Reales. s/n. © **95-742-01-51.** Admission 4.50€ adults, 2€ students, free ages 1–13, free for all Tues–Fri 8:30–9:30am. Sound and light spectacle 7€ adults, 4.80€ seniors. Tues–Fri 8:30am–8:45pm, Sat 8:30am–4:30pm, Sun 8:30am–2pm. Bus: 3 or 12.

Casa Andalusí ★ MUSEUM A small fountain strewn with roses welcomes visitors to the ivy-draped main courtyard of this small museum, which tries to re-create daily life in Córdoba during the 12th-century caliphate. Don't spend too much time studying the model of the mill on the Río Guadalquivír, which produced paper for spiritual texts, or reading the often heavy-handed interpretive notes. Instead, take a seat on a low chair, lean against an embroidered cushion, breathe in the scent of the flowers, and listen to the gurgle of the fountain.

Calle Judíos, 12. © **95-729-06-42.** www.lacasaandalusi.com. Admission 2.50€. Daily 10am–7pm. Bus: 3, 12.

Casa Sefarad ★ MUSEUM This small museum focuses on 11th- and 12th-century daily Jewish life in Córdoba, the de facto capital of Sephardic Jewry. The rooms with the most resonance explicate the traditional craft of making golden thread, highlight Sephardic musical and literary traditions, and celebrate

INSIDE THE blooming PATIOS

The middle of May is not the time to visit Córdoba for the climate (it's already scorching hot), but it is the season for meeting Córdobans inside their homes. They are so proud of the flowers that they grow in their patios that many of them open to visitors for the **Concurso de los Patios de Córdoba,** or **Córdoba Patio Festival** (www.amigos delospatioscordobeses.es). Pick up a map of participants from the tourist office. When you enter people's homes, you will see their ancient patios arranged around a well or fountain with whitewashed walls hung with pots of blazing geraniums, or *gitanillas* ("little Gypsies"). Admission is free, but it's customary to leave a few coins in a tip tray to help with upkeep.

If you miss the patio festival, you can still get an idea of the patios so central to Córdoban life by visiting the **Palacio Museo de Viana ★**, Plaza de Don Gome, 2 (© **95-749-67-41;** www.palaciode viana.com), which is 4 blocks southeast of the Plaza de Colón just outside the Judería. The interior is of most interest to fans of decorative arts, but the 12 patios, representing various eras and architectural styles, are an uplifting sight for all. It's open July to August Tuesday to Sunday 9am to 2pm and 7 to 10pm; September to June Tuesday to Saturday 10am to 7pm, Sunday 10am to 3pm.

Christian, Jewish, and Islamic women of Córdoba's heyday who were leading poets, philosophers, singers, and scholars.

Corner of calles Judíos and Averroes. © **95-742-14-04.** www. casadesefarad.com. Admission 4€ adults, 3€ students. Mon–Sat 11am–6pm; Sun 11am–2pm. Bus: 3, 12.

Mezquita Catedral de Córdoba ★★★ MOSQUE From the 8th to 11th centuries, the Mezquita was the crowning architectural achievement of western Islam.

It's a fantastic forest of arches painted with alternating red and white stripes—a realization in stone of a billowing desert tent. A Roman Catholic cathedral interrupts the vistas, as it sits awkwardly in the middle of the mosque as an enduring symbol of Christian hubris. The 16th-century cathedral may have been architectural sacrilege, but it does have an intricately carved ceiling and baroque choir stalls. One of the interesting features of the mosque is the *mihrab* ★★, a domed shrine of Byzantine mosaics that once housed the Qu'ran. After exploring the interior, stroll through the Patio de los Naranjos (Courtyard of the Orange Trees), which has a beautiful fountain where worshippers performed their ablutions before prayer and tourists rest their weary feet.

Calles Torrijos and Cardenal Herrero s/n (southeast of the train station, just north of the Roman bridge). ✆ **95-822-52-45.** www. mezquitadecordoba.org. Admission 8€ adults, 4€ children 14

The Patio de los Naranjos (Courtyard of the Orange Trees) at Mezquita Catedral de Córdoba.

and under. Mon–Sat 10am–6pm; Sun 9–10:30am and 2–6pm. Bus: 3.

Museo Arqueológico de Córdoba ★★ MUSEUM

The new museum building for this well-established collection of artifacts opened in 2011 next door to the 1505 palace that had hosted the museum for more than a century. The site was originally a Roman amphitheater, and intact portions of the theater were found and have been revealed in the basement of the new structure. This museum chronicles life in and around Córdoba since the first Neandertals came to the area 300,000 years ago. Those first residents left no artifacts of note, but more recent inhabitants did. Displays of tools and household items begin with Copper and Bronze Age cultures, followed by Phoenician and Greek artifacts, Iberian statuary (circa 500 B.C.), and extensive Roman materials. The Moorish artifacts, of course, are legion. The old home of the museum is closed until further notice, pending an improvement in the economy that will allow restoration.

Plaza Jerónimo Páez, 7. © **95-735-55-17.** www.museosdean dalucia.es. Admission 1.50€. Tues 2:30–8:30pm; Wed–Sat 9am–8:30pm; Sun 9am–2:30pm. Bus: 3.

Sinagoga ★ SYNAGOGUE

Córdoba boasts one of Spain's three remaining pre-Inquisition synagogues, built in 1315, two blocks west of the northern wall of La Mezquita (p. 43). The synagogue is noted particularly for its stuccowork, including Mudéjar patterns on the entrance and Hebrew inscriptions from the Psalms inside. The east wall contains a large orifice where the Tabernacle was placed (the scrolls of the Pentateuch were kept inside), and you can still see the balcony where women worshipped. After Spain expelled the

A CALIPH'S pleasure PALACE

Conjunto Arqueológico Madinat al-Zahra ★, a kind of Moorish Versailles just outside Córdoba, was constructed in the 10th century by the first caliph of al-Andalus, Abd ar-Rahman III. He named it after the favorite of his harem, nicknamed "the brilliant." Thousands of workers and animals slaved to build this mammoth pleasure palace, said to have contained 300 baths and 400 houses. Over the years the site was plundered for building materials; some of its materials may have been used to build the Alcázar in Sevilla. The Royal House, a rendezvous point for the ministers, has been reconstructed. The principal salon remains in fragments, though, so you have to imagine it in its majesty. Just beyond the Royal House are the ruins of a mosque constructed to face Mecca. The Berbers sacked the palace in 1013 when the Umayyad dynasty briefly took control of al-Andalus.

The palace is at Carretera Palma de Río, Km 8 (**℃ 95-735-28-74**; www.museosde-andalucia.es). Admission is 1.50€ (free to E.U. residents). From mid-September to March, hours are Tuesday to Saturday 9am to 6:30pm, Sunday 10am to 5pm; in April and May, hours are Tuesday to Saturday 9am to 8pm, Sunday 10am to 5pm; June to mid-September Tuesday to Saturday 10am to 3:30pm, and Sunday 10am to 5pm. Two buses a day leave from Avenida del Alcázar and Paseo de la Victoria (**℃ 95-735-51-79**). The roundtrip bus costs 8.50€ adults, 4.25€ ages 5 to 12. Tickets are sold at the tourist office.

Jews in 1492, the synagogue was converted into a hospital, then in 1588, a Catholic chapel.
Calle de los Judíos 20. *℃* **95-720-29-28.** Admission 0.30€. Tues–Sun 9am–2:30pm. Bus: 3.

Torre de la Calahorra ★ MUSEUM   As you cross the Puente Romano (constructed in the reign of Julius

Caesar and rebuilt many times since), you'll see herons and egrets wading in the shallows and worshippers crossing themselves and leaving sprigs of rosemary at a small shrine to the archangel San Rafael at the midpoint of the bridge. The display rooms at the Torre are often crowded with school groups, so arrive early. The 1-hour audio tour evokes Córdoba of the 9th to 13th centuries, and is as valuable for vacationers as it is for kids studying history. One room features likenesses of some of Córdoba's great thinkers, including Averroes, Maimonides, and Alfonso X.

Av. de la Confederación, Puente Romano. ✆ **95-729-39-29.** www.torrecalahorra.com. Admission to museum 4.50€ adults, 3€ seniors and students, free ages 8 and under. May–Sept daily 10am–2pm and 4:30–8:30pm; Oct–Apr daily 10am–6pm. Tours daily 11am, noon, 3, and 4pm. Bus: 16.

Shopping

As you walk through the streets of the Judería, you would practically have to wear blinders not to be tempted by the merchandise in the shops, which ranges from tourist trinkets to flamenco-inspired jewelry and shawls to Moorish-inspired textiles, inlaid boxes, and glass tea cups. If you want to concentrate your shopping in one place, check **Arte Zoco,** Calle de Los Judíos, s/n (✆ **95-729-05-75**), a charming courtyard reached through an arched entry. The site boasts a shop and about a dozen stalls where artists sell jewelry and pottery, along with work in wood, leather, and other materials. Alas, the artists keep irregular hours, but it's worth stopping in for the opportunity to buy a memento of Córdoba from its maker.

4

GRANADA

When Boabdil, the last king of Moorish Granada, was exiled to North Africa in 1492, he took the bones of his ancestors with him. But he left behind their fortress-palace, the Alhambra, and a legacy of nearly 8 centuries of Islamic culture. Fernando and Isabel may have won the war and completed the reconquest of al-Andalus, but in Granada they lost the history. Few people come to this beautiful city to see the solemn tombs of Los Reyes Católicos. They come for the joyous ornamentation of the Alhambra, the inextinguishably Arabic face of the Albaícin, and the haunting *zambras* echoing from the Sacromonte hills. As native son Federico García Lorca wrote, "Oh city of gypsies! Who could see you and not remember?"

Essentials

GETTING THERE **Iberia** (© **800/772-4642** in the U.S., or 90-240-05-00 toll-free in Spain; www.iberia.com) flies to Granada from Madrid four times daily. **Vueling** (© **80-720-01-00** from within Spain; www.vueling.com) has three direct flights a day from

PREVIOUS PAGE: **Sunlight streams through a door of the Alhambra.**

Barcelona to Granada. Granada's **Federico García Lorca Airport** (*aeropuerto nacional*) is 16km (10 miles) west of the center of town on Carretera Málaga; call ✆ **90-240-47-04** for information. A bus route links the airport with the center of Granada. The one-way fare is 3€. The bus runs daily 5:30am to 8pm. Trip time is 45 minutes.

The **train** station is **Estación de RENFE de Granada,** Av. Andaluces s/n (✆ **90-232-03-20;** www. renfe.es). Granada is well linked with the most important Spanish cities, especially others in Andalucía. Four trains daily arrive from Sevilla, taking 3 to 4 hours, depending on the train, and costing 25€ one-way. From Madrid, two daily trains arrive, taking 4½ hours and costing 68€.

Granada is served by more **buses** than trains. It has links to virtually all the major towns and cities in Andalucía, and even to Madrid. The main bus terminal is **Estación de Autobuses de Granada,** Carretera de Jaén s/n (✆ **95-818-54-80**). One of the most heavily used bus routes is the one between Sevilla and Granada, with 10 buses run per day, costing 19€ for a one-way ticket. The trip is 3 hours. You can also reach Granada in 3 hours on one of nine daily buses from Córdoba; cost is 14€ for a one-way ticket. If you're on the Costa del Sol, the run is just 2 hours, costing 12€ per one-way ticket. This is a very popular route, with 19 buses going back and forth between Granada and the coast per day. For bus information, contact **Alsa** (✆ **95-818-54-80;** www.alsa.es).

GETTING AROUND   Just a few buses will take you pretty much anywhere you want to go in Granada. The 30 and 32 city buses (1.50€) run continuously from Plaza Isabel la Catolica to the ticket office of the

Alhambra, and the 31 and 32 buses leave from the same spot for Sacromonte. Taxis are relatively inexpensive.

VISITOR INFORMATION The **Patronato Provincial de Turismo de Granada,** Plaza de Mariana Pineda, 10 (© **95-824-71-46;** www.turgranada.es), is open Monday to Friday 9am to 8pm, Saturday 10am to 7pm, and Sunday 10am to 3pm. For information on both the city and surrounding area, the **Tourist Information Office of Junta de Andalucía,** Calle de Santa Ana. 4 (© **95-857-52-02;** www.andalucia.org), is open Monday to Friday 9am to 7:30pm, Saturday and Sunday 9:30am to 3pm. Two big festivals dominate the agenda—the **International Theater Festival,** which attracts avant-garde theater groups from around the world, and the **Festival Internacional de Música y Danza.**

Where to Stay
EXPENSIVE
AC Palacio de Santa Paula ★★★   This adaptation of the 16th-century Convento de Santa Paula and a 12th-century Moorish palace bridges the historic structures with an ultra-modern steel and glass shell. The ambiance of the earlier buildings is maintained in some of the public areas, including the beautiful courtyard of the cloister. Rooms are cool and modern, with ample space. Standard rooms have no particular view, while superior rooms overlook the Moorish courtyard and some deluxe rooms look up at the Alhambra. The Palacio de Santa Paula is Granada's most luxurious hotel, rivaled only by the *parador* on the Alhambra grounds (see below).

Gran Vía de Colón, 31. © **95-880-57-40.** www.palaciodesanta paula.com. 75 units. 125€–215€ double; 209€-240€ jr. suite. Parking 18€ per day. Bus: 3, 6, 8, or 11. **Amenities:** Restaurant; bar; exercise room; sauna; free Wi-Fi.

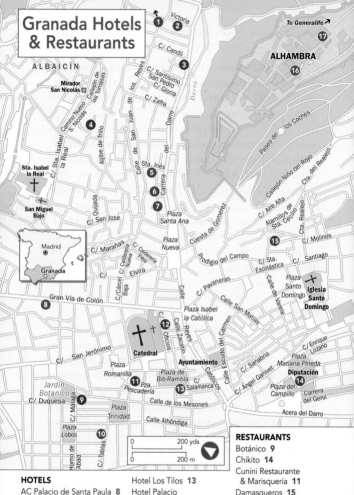

Granada Hotels & Restaurants

ALBAICÍN

Victoria ①②

C/ Candil

C/ Santisimo
San Pedro
C/ Gloria. ③

C/ Zafra

Mirador San Nicolás ▣

Callejón de las Tomasas

Camino Nuevo S. Nicolás

C/ Sta. Isabel la Real

Aljibe de Trillo

Calle de San Juan de los Reyes

Sta. Isabel la Real ✝

San Miguel Bajo ✝

C/ Quijada

C/ San José

C/ Marañas

C/ Calderería Nueva

C/ Calderería Vieja

C/ Cárcel Baja

Elvira

Gran Vía de Colón ⑧

Darro

C/ Sta. Inés ⑤
⑥
⑦

Carrera del Darro

Plaza Santa Ana

Plaza Nueva

Cuesta de Gomérez

Prodigio del Campo

C/ Pavaneras

Calle San Matías

Calle Reyes

To Generalife ↗ ⑰

ALHAMBRA ⑯

Paseo de los Coches

Callejón Niño del Rojo

Cta. del Realejo

C/ Aire Alta

Alamillos de Sta. Cecilio

Cta. Realejo

C/ Molinos ⑮

C/ Sta. Escolástica

C/ Santiago

Plaza Santo Domingo

Calle de Varela

Iglesia Santo Domingo ✝

Madrid
Granada

C/ San Jerónimo

Plaza Romanilla

Catedral ✝

⑫

Plaza de Bib-Rambla

Pza. Pescadería ⑪

C/ Oficios

Calle Zacatín

Ayuntamiento

C/ Salamanca ⑬

Calle de los Mesones

Plaza Isabel la Católica

Calle Escudo del Carmen

Calle San Matías

C/ Sanabria

C/ Ángel Ganivet

C/ Enrique Lozano

Plaza Mariana Pineda

Diputación ⑭

Plaza del Campillo

Carrera del Genil

Acera del Darro

Jardín Botánico ⑨

C/ Duquesa

C/ Málaga

C/ Tablas

Horno de Abad

Plaza Trinidad

Calle Alhóndiga

Plaza Lobos ⑩

| 0 | 200 yds |
| 0 | 200 m |

HOTELS

AC Palacio de Santa Paula **8**
Casa del Capitel Nazarí **6**
Casa Morisca **2**
Hotel América **16**
Hotel Casa 1800 **7**

Hotel Los Tilos **13**
Hotel Palacio de Santa Inés **5**
Hotel Reina Cristina **10**
Las Cuevas El Abanico **1**
Parador de Granada **17**

RESTAURANTS

Botánico **9**
Chikito **14**
Cunini Restaurante & Marisquería **11**
Damasqueros **15**
El Huerto de Juan Ranas **4**
Restaurante Ruta del Azafrán **3**
Restaurante Sevilla **12**

MODERATE

Casa Morisca ★★   Lovingly restored by a Madrid architect, this traditional 16th-century house in the Alabaicín retains its central patio and Moorish fountain, its rough brickwork, its columns with Nasrid capitals, and its narrow view of the Alhambra from the "Mirador" room, which is a suite that costs a lot more than smaller rooms. The Granadino style, so influenced by the decoration of the Alhambra and lingering links with North Africa, carries through in all the decorations. Some parking is available but must be arranged ahead to get a permit to bring the car to the property. Cuesta de la Victoria, 9. © **95-822-11-00.** www.hotelcasamorisca. com. 14 units. 86€–170€ double; 155€–220€ suite. Free parking. Bus: 31 or 32. **Amenities:** Free Wi-Fi.

Hotel Palacio de Santa Inés ★★   A pioneer in transforming the neighborhood's Mudéjar homes into lodgings for tourists, the Palacio de Santa Inés opened in the mid-1990s. The courtyard architecture and beamed ceilings evoke the building's origins as two private homes. The hotel takes its design cues from the fragmentary 16th-century frescoes in the reception area. Rooms and public areas are decorated throughout with bold hues of Tuscan plaster. Interior balconies with wooden spindles circle the courtyard. Several rooms have partial views of the Alhambra. Reserve well in advance. Cuesta de Santa Inés, 9. © **95-822-23-62.** www.palaciosanta ines.com. 35 units. 60€–145€ double; 145€–225€ suite. Parking 19€. Bus: 30 or 32. **Amenities:** Afternoon tea; free Wi-Fi.

Hotel Reina Cristina ★   Mildly famous as the house where Federico García Lorca was last seen alive when he was abducted by Franco's thugs, this former grand family home has become a charming hotel in the middle of the city. It's only a 5-minute stroll to the cathedral.

STAYING ON THE alhambra GROUNDS

It's not quite the same as staying in one of the rooms of the Alhambra itself, but there are two lodgings—one extremely luxurious, the other more modest—located inside the walls of the palace complex. If you'd like to wander the grounds after the other tourists have gone home, plan to reserve a room far in advance, but keep in mind that both lodgings are inconvenient for visiting the rest of Granada.

The **Parador de Granada ★★★**, Real de Alhambra, s/n (*C* **95-822-14-40;** www. parador.es) is the harder nut to crack. Its 36 rooms are decorated to reflect the architectural and decorative style of the Alhambra, and it's one of the most luxurious stays in Spain. Try for a room in the

atmospheric older section. Double room rates begin at 320€ per night, suites at 618€. For those prices you do get free Wi-Fi.

The **Hotel América ★★**, Real de Alhambra s/n (*C* **95-822-74-71;** www.hotel americagranada.com), is a former private home converted in 1936 into an intimate hotel with just 17 small rooms decorated in intense warm colors with sponged walls, hand-painted headboards, and rustic touches like unpainted wood doors and window frames. Some rooms overlook a patio garden with a grape pergola, while others look out on the gardens of the Alhambra Palace. Double room rates range from 110€ to 140€. They also include free Wi-Fi.

Guest rooms are modest in size and furnished in a simple, rather old-fashioned style with floral bedspreads and striped curtains.

Calle Tablas, 4. *C* **95-825-32-11.** www.hotelreinacristina.com. 56 units. 58€–153€ double; 73€–168€ triple. Parking 18€. Bus: 5. **Amenities:** Restaurant; bar; free Wi-Fi.

Casa del Capitel Nazarí ★   Skip the supplement for a room with a view of the Alhambra, since the view is seriously obstructed and the hotel is worth enjoying in its own right. The lodging takes its name from the original Nasrid capital that helps support the 16th-century building. Historic preservation precluded an elevator, but ground-floor rooms are available. Bathrooms are equipped with showers rather than tubs to maximize the living space in the chambers. The rooms have carved wooden ceilings in the Nasrid style, and minibars—a luxury that even the emirs didn't enjoy. Cuesta Aceituneros, 6. ✆ **95-821-52-60.** www.hotelcasacapitel. com. 18 units. 60€–135€ double. Bus: 5, 11, 31, 32. **Amenities:** Free Wi-Fi.

Hotel Casa 1800 ★★   Sister to the property by the same name in Sevilla (p. 10), this pretty and welcoming hotel is tucked into a small cul-de-sac off Plaza Nueva, making the location both convenient yet surprisingly quiet. The decorative style is a kind of baroque revival, with lots of curlicue flourishes in the decorative painting and a palette of browns, tans, and golds. Standard rooms are quite snug, but feature queen-size beds. Superior and deluxe rooms have either two twins or a king. Several rooms have exposed brick walls and exposed beams on the ceilings. Calle Benalúa, 11. ✆ **95-821-08-00.** www.hotelcasa1800.com. 25 rooms. 75€–215€ double; 135€–295€ jr. suite. Bus: 5, 11. **Amenities:** Afternoon tea; free Wi-Fi.

INEXPENSIVE

Hotel Los Tilos ★   It helps to enjoy the company of fellow travelers if you opt for Los Tilos: The elevator is tight and guests congregate on the top-floor balcony, where it's fun to spend an evening with a bottle of wine and good company. Rooms are large at this price and are brightly painted in luminous yellows, oranges, and tropical marine blue. Of the hotel's 30 rooms, 22 have views of the lovely plaza filled with good tapas bars and cafes. Location in the heart of city and the availability of triple rooms (good for families) are big pluses. Book three or more nights to get free breakfast.

Plaza Bib-Rambla, 4. ✆ **95-826-67-12.** www.hotellostilos.com. 30 rooms. 40€–70€ double. Bus: 23, 30, 31, 32. **Amenities:** Free Wi-Fi in public areas.

Las Cuevas El Abanico ★   As much an adventure as a lodging, these one- and two-bedroom units in the Gypsy quarter of Sacromonte are fully modernized cave dwellings with whitewashed walls, tiny bathrooms, and a corner equipped for minimal cooking. The kids won't be able to wait to tell their friends they stayed in a Gypsy cave. You, too. Just be aware that the caves are a real uphill schlep from the road and there is a cleaning fee charged when you check out. Most units are rented by the week.

Calle Verea de Enmedio, 89. ✆ **95-822-61-99.** www.el-abanico. com. 5 units. 1-bedroom 68€ per night, 420€ per week; 2-bedroom 110€ per night, 660€ per week. Bus: 35.

Where to Eat

EXPENSIVE

Damasqueros ★★ ANDALUCIAN   Having trained with some of the top names in Spanish cooking (Berasategui and Subijana among them), Lola Marin opened this handsome restaurant in the new part of town in late 2009 and quickly won a dedicated following among Granada gastronomes. Marin cooks from her Andalucían roots, drawing on Jewish and Moorish influences, but she presents the dishes in a carefully edited fashion that could grace the cover of any food magazine. Her barely cooked foie gras, for example, is accompanied by chocolate popcorn and sweet-and-sour quince paste. Her garlic and saffron-infused rice "soup" that's halfway to a risotto is studded with asparagus tips and topped with shaved truffles. She roasts lamb with whole grapes and serves it with fried bread crumbs and melon. It's anyone's guess what she'll be cooking next week, but a peek on the website will tell you what's being served tonight. Damasqueros serves just one menu per day, with or without a wine pairing.

Calle Damasqueros, 3. ℂ **95-821-05-50.** www.damasqueros. com. Tasting menu 40€, with wine pairing 59€. Tues–Sat 1–4:30pm and 8–11:30pm, Sun 1–4:30pm. Closed mid-July to Aug.

El Huerto de Juan Ranas ★ ANDALUCIAN Chef-owner Juan Ranas is a romantic when it comes to dining, and his "garden" at one corner of the Mirador San Nicolás assumes a kind of fairytale elegance once the candles are lit. He serves an excellent tapas menu in the garden terrace upstairs, including his creamy croquettes. The downstairs dining room with linen-clad tables and a profusion of glassware features an updated version of Andalucían classics. The roast lamb shoulder, for example, is cooked slowly at a very low temperature until it falls apart, and the Moorish pastries combine small pieces of fork-tender meat as well as chunks of eggplant.

Calle de Atarazana, 8 (Mirador de San Nicolás). ℂ **95-828-69-25.** www.elhuertodejuanranas.com. Main courses 19€–40€. Fixed-price menus 45€–57€. Daily 8–11:30pm. Bus: 31.

MODERATE

Chikito ★ SPANISH Once upon a time, this spot was the location of the bar-restaurant Alameda, where Federico García Lorca and the rest of the literary circle known as El Rinconcillo used to meet up in the 1920s and trade verses and songs. Should he suddenly materialize, Lorca would probably find the food unchanged from those days. Chef Antonio Torres does an intense version of roast cod with mint and the warm spices of North Africa as well as desserts that feature pastry, nuts, and honey. The plaza is as pleasant as it was in Lorca's day, so that's where most people sit.

Plaza del Campillo 9. ⓒ **95-822-33-64.** www.restaurante chikito.com. Main courses 12€–30€. Daily menu 25€. Thurs–Tues 1–4pm and 8–11:30pm. Bus: 1, 2, or 7.

Cunini Restaurante & Marisquería ★★★ SEAFOOD   If there is one dining scene in Granada that you should not miss, it is eating seafood tapas at Cunini. Granada restaurants are extraordinarily generous with free tapas, and Cunini is more generous than most. You can sample much of the menu here by standing at the undulating marble bar and ordering drink after drink. (The tapas get better with each drink, and that's not the alcohol talking.) If you want to enjoy the best seafood in Granada, have a seat in the restaurant or on the plaza for the likes of monkfish in white wine or a heaping plate of fried red mullet.

Plaza de Pescadería, 14. ⓒ **95-825-07-77.** www.marisqueria cunini.es. Main courses 13€–33€. Mon–Sat noon–2am. Bus: 23, 30, 31, 32.

INEXPENSIVE

Botánico ★ MEDITERRANEAN   Located on a small plaza west of the cathedral near the university's law school, Botánico wears many different hats through the day and night. Most of the time it's a bright and cheery cafe-bar where you can get tapas and a beer or a coffee, though it also serves a full, inexpensive dinner menu of Mediterranean and Indian fare. Local artists hang their works on the walls for sale. Around 11pm on weekends, the lights dim, the techno music blasts, and folks start dancing.

Calle Málaga, 3. ☏ **95-827-15-98.** http://botanicocafe.es/en Reservations recommended. Main courses 7.90€–30€; daily menu 15€. Daily 1pm–2am. Bus: 4, 7, or 13.

Restaurante Ruta del Azafrán ★ ANDALUCIAN Contemporary Spanish cooking with a decidedly North African accent is only half the attraction here. There are also great views (looking up) of the Alhambra, and a range of menu choices from inexpensive couscous to veal steaks with foie gras. Most plates are intended to be light and bright, and there are a number of salad entrees at lunch. The wine list includes some bargains on local white table wines as well as a great selection of bottles from some of Spain's emerging wine regions, such as Jumilla.

Paseo del Padre Manjón, 1. ☏ **95-822-68-82.** www.rutadel azafran.com. Main courses 9€–22€. Sun–Thurs 1–4pm, 8–11; Fri–Sat1–4pm, 8pm–midnight. Bus: 31.

Restaurante Sevilla ★ SPANISH   Now run by the Alvarez brothers (Dany the chef and Jorge the maître d'), this old-fashioned favorite sits on a tiny street near the cathedral. So modest is the entrance that you might hear a guitarist playing a Manuel de Falla tune before you find the door. But Restaurante Sevilla has been Granada's see-and-be-seen venue since the 1930s, when de Falla and poet Federico García Lorca used to eat here. The staff pushes the gazpacho, but we suggest the Andalucían lamb with mountain herbs, *cordero a la pastoril*. In season, make reservations.

Calle Oficios, 12. ☏ **95-822-12-23.** www.restaurantesevilla.es. Main courses 12€–26€; tasting menu 36€. Tues–Sat 1–4:30pm and 8–11:30pm. Bus: 32 or 39.

Exploring Granada

One school of thought about visiting Granada says that after seeing the Alhambra you can die happy and need not bestir yourself to see anything else. But Granada is one of the most interesting and sociable cities in Spain, and it would be a pity if you overlooked any of it. After you've visited the Alhambra, spend at least a full day (and evening) to savor the rest.

The **Puerta de Elvira** is the gate through which Fernando and Isabel made their triumphant entry into Granada in 1492 after the last Moorish ruler, Boabdil, fled. It was once a grisly place where the rotting heads of executed criminals hung from its portals. The quarter surrounding the gate was the Muslim section (*morería*) until all Muslims were forced to convert or leave the country about a century after the Reconquest.

One of the more colorful streets is **Calle de Elvira;** west of it, the medieval residential neighborhood of the Albaicín rises on a hill. (Granada's modern mosque is in this quarter.) In the 17th and 18th centuries, many artisans occupied the shops and ateliers along Elvira and its side streets. The **Iglesia de San Andrés,** begun in 1528, and its Mudéjar bell tower are also on Calle de Elvira. Much of the church was destroyed by fire in the early 19th century, but several interesting paintings and sculptures remain. Another old church in this area is the **Iglesia de Santiago,** constructed in 1501 and dedicated to St. James the Apostle, patron saint of Spain. Built on the site of an Arab mosque, it was damaged in an 1884 earthquake. The church contains the tomb of architect Diego de Siloé (1495–1563), who did much to change the face of the city.

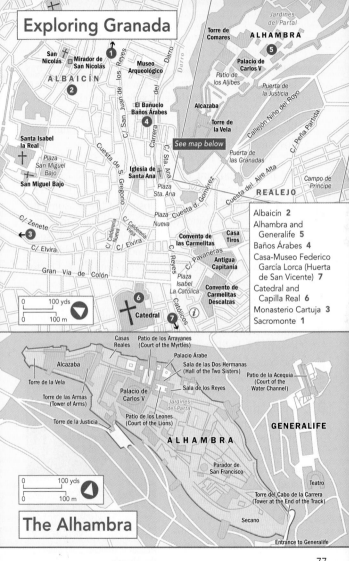

Exploring Granada

ALHAMBRA

Torre de Comares

Jardines del Partal

San Nicolás
Mirador de San Nicolás

Museo Arqueológico

ALBAICÍN

Palacio de Carlos V

Patio de los Aljibes

Puerta de la Justicia

El Bañuelo Baños Árabes

Alcazaba

Torre de la Vela

Callejón Niño del Royo

C/ Peña Partida

See map below

Santa Isabel la Real

Plaza San Miguel Bajo

San Miguel Bajo

Puerta de las Granadas

Iglesia de Santa Ana

Plaza Sta. Ana

Campo de Príncipe

Cuesta del Aire Alta

REALEJO

C/ Zenete

Cuesta d. Gomérez

Plaza Nueva

C/ Elvira

Gran Via de Colón

Convento de las Carmelitas

Casa Tiros

Antigua Capitania

Plaza Isabel La Católica

Convento de Carmelitas Descalzas

Catedral

Albaicín **2**
Alhambra and Generalife **5**
Baños Árabes **4**
Casa-Museo Federico García Lorca (Huerta de San Vicente) **7**
Catedral and Capilla Real **6**
Monasterio Cartuja **3**
Sacromonte **1**

0 — 100 yds
0 — 100 m

The Alhambra

Casas Reales

Patio de los Arrayanes (Court of the Myrtles)

Palacio Árabe

Sala de las Dos Hermanas (Hall of the Two Sisters)

Alcazaba

Palacio de Carlos V

Sala de los Reyes

Jardines del Partal

Patio de la Acequia (Court of the Water Channel)

Torre de la Vela

Torre de las Armas (Tower of Arms)

Torre de la Justicia

Patio de los Leones (Court of the Lions)

GENERALIFE

ALHAMBRA

Parador de San Francisco

Teatro

Torre del Cabo de la Carrera (Tower at the End of the Track)

Secano

Entrance to Generalife

0 — 100 yds
0 — 100 m

Despite its name, the oldest extant square in Granada is **Plaza Nueva,** which, under the Muslims, was the site of the woodcutters' bridge. The Darro has been covered over here, but its waters still flow underneath the square. On the east side of Plaza is the 16th-century Iglesia de Santa Ana, built by Siloé. Inside its five-nave interior you can see Churrigueresque reredos and a coffered ceiling.

The *corrida* has a valiant history in Granada, with the most important bullfights taking place from the 3rd week of May through the 3rd week of June. The final Sunday of September closes out the season with a special card in honor of the Virgen de las Angustias, Granada's patron saint. The 1928 bullring seats 14,500, so there are usually good seats available. The **Plaza de Toros,** the bullring, is on Avenida de Doctor Olóriz, close to the soccer stadium.

Albaicín ★★ NEIGHBORHOOD   This old quarter on one of Granada's two main hills stands apart from the city of 19th-century buildings and wide boulevards. A holdover from the Nasrid empire, it even predates the Renaissance city that sprung up around the cathedral. The Albaicín and Gypsy caves of Sacromonte farther up the hill (see below) were the homes of marginalized Muslims and Gypsies declared beyond the pale by the Christian conquerors. The narrow labyrinth of crooked streets in

Houses in Granada's old quarter, the Albaicín.

the Albaicín was too hilly to tear down in the name of progress; ironically, it is now some of the most desirable real estate in Granada. Its alleyways, cisterns, fountains, plazas, whitewashed houses, villas, and the decaying remnants of the old city gate have all been preserved. Here and there you can catch a glimpse of a private patio filled with fountains and plants, a traditional, elegant way of life that continues. The plaza known as **Mirador San Nicolás** is a delightful spot to enjoy a drink at a cafe. It becomes especially romantic at sunset, when the reflected color makes the Alhambra seem to glow on the opposite hill. During the winter and spring, you may even see snow on the peaks of the Sierra Nevada mountains.

Bus: 31 or 32.

Alhambra and Generalife ★★★ PALACE   One of Europe's greatest attractions, the stunningly beautiful and celebrated **Calat Alhambra (Red Castle)** is perhaps the most remarkable fortress ever constructed. Muslim architecture in Spain reached its apogee at this palace once occupied by Nasrid princes, their families, and their political and personal functionaries. Although the Alhambra was converted into a lavish palace in the 13th and 14th centuries, it was originally constructed for defensive purposes on a rocky hilltop outcropping above the Darro River. The modern city of Granada was built across the river from the Alhambra, about 0.8km (½ mile) from its western foundations.

When you first see the Alhambra, its somewhat somber exterior may surprise you. The true delights of this Moorish palace lie within. If you haven't already purchased your ticket, they are sold in the office at the Entrada del Generalife y de la Alhambra. Enter through the incongruous 14th-century **Puerta de la Justicia (Gateway of Justice)** ★. Most visitors do not need an expensive guide but will be content to stroll through the richly ornamented open-air rooms, with lace-like walls and courtyards with fountains. Many of the Arabic inscriptions translate to "Only Allah is conqueror."

The strictly defined pathway of the tour begins in the **Mexuar** ★★★, also known as Palacio Nazaríes (Palace of the Nasrids), which is the first of three palaces that compose the Alhambra. This was the main council chamber where the chief ministers met. The largest of these chambers was the Hall of the Mexuar, which Spanish rulers converted to a Catholic chapel in the 1600s. From this chapel, there's a panoramic view over the rooftops of the Albaicín.

Detailed mosaic work in the Alhambra.

reserving **FOR THE ALHAMBRA**

The Alhambra is so popular that the government has limited the number of people who can enter each day and has limited the number of tickets purchased by one individual to 10 per day. The best way to enjoy the Alhambra is to arrive first thing in the morning and proceed to the Nasrid Palaces as soon as possible (you must enter the palaces at the specific time on your ticket). To avoid long ticket lines, buy your tickets in advance. The easiest way is to order online at www.

alhambra-tickets.es, or by calling ☎ **95-892-60-31**. Tickets can also be purchased (or picked up) at the Tienda de la Alhambra, Calle Reyes Católicos, 40 in the city center. They may also be picked up at the vending machines at the Alhambra entrance. You will need identification to secure your tickets, but once you have them in hand you can bypass the lines and proceed to the entrance. All advance purchases carry a small (1.3%) surcharge, which is well worth it.

Pass through another chamber of the sultan's ministers, the Cuarto Dorado (Golden Room), and you'll find yourself in the small but beautiful **Patio del Mexuar ★★**. Constructed in 1365, this is where the emir sat on giant cushions and listened to the petitions of his subjects, or met privately with his chief ministers. The windows here are surrounded by panels and richly decorated with tiles and stucco.

The Palace of the Nasrids was constructed around two courtyards, the **Patio de los Arrayanes (Court of the Myrtles) ★★** and the **Patio de los Leones (Court of the Lions) ★★★**. The latter was the royal residence.

The Court of the Myrtles contains a narrow reflecting pool banked by myrtle trees. Note the decorative and rather rare tiles, which are arguably the finest in the Alhambra. Behind it is the **Salón de Embajadores (Hall of the Ambassadors) ★★**, with an elaborately carved throne room that was built between 1334 and 1354. The crowning cedar wood dome of this salon evokes the seven heavens of the Muslim cosmos. Here bay windows open onto **panoramic vistas** of the enveloping countryside.

An opening off the Court of the Myrtles leads to the greatest architectural achievement of the Alhambra, the Patio de los Leones (Court of Lions), constructed by Muhammad V. At its center is Andalucía's finest fountain, which rests on 12 marble lions. The lions represent the hours of the day, the months of the year, and the signs of the zodiac. Legend claims that water flowed from the mouth of a different lion each hour of the day. This courtyard is lined with arcades supported by 124 (count them) slender marble columns. This was the heart of the palace, the private section where the emir and his family retreated.

At the back of the Leones courtyard is the **Sala de los Abencerrajes ★**, named for a noble family whom 16th-century legend says were slaughtered here, either because they were political rivals of the emir, or because one of them was sleeping with the emir's wife. It makes a terrific tale, but there is no historical evidence to support it.

Opening onto the Court of Lions are other salons of intrigue, notably the Hall of the Two Sisters, **Sala de las Dos Hermanas ★★**, which is named for the two identical large white marble slabs in the pavement. Boabdil's stern, unforgiving mother, Ayesha, once inhabited the Hall of the Two Sisters. This salon has a stunning dome of carved plaster and is often cited as one of the finest examples of Spanish Islamic architecture.

The nearby **Sala de los Reyes (Hall of Kings)** ★ was the great banquet hall of the Alhambra. Its ceiling paintings are on leather and date from the 1300s. A gallery leads to the **Patio de la Reja (Court of the Window Grille)** ★. This is where Washington Irving lived in furnished rooms, and where he began to write his famous book *Tales of the Alhambra*. The best-known tale is the legend of Zayda, Zorayda, and Zorahayda, the three beautiful princesses who fell in love with three captured Spanish soldiers outside the Torre de las Infantas. Irving credits the French with saving the Alhambra for posterity, but in fact they were responsible for blowing up seven of the towers in 1812, and it was a Spanish soldier who cut the fuse before more damage could be done. When the Duke of Wellington arrived a few years later, he chased out the chickens, the Gypsies, and the transient beggars who were squatting in the Alhambra and set up housekeeping here himself.

Before you proceed to the Emperor Carlos V's palace, look at some other gems around the Court of Lions, including the **Baños Reales (Royal Baths)** ★, with their lavish, multicolored decorations. Light enters through star-shaped apertures. To the immediate east of the baths lies the **Daraxa Garden** ★, and to its immediate south the lovely and resplendent **Mirador de Daraxa** ★★, the sultana's private balcony onto Granada.

To the immediate southeast of these attractions are the **Jardines del Partal** ★★ and their perimeter towers. These beautiful gardens occupy a space that once was the kitchen garden, filled with milling servants preparing the sultan's banquets. These gardens are dominated by the **Torre de Las Damas (Ladies' Tower)** ★.

This tower and its pavilion, with its five-arched porticoes, are all that are left of the once-famous Palacio del Partal, the oldest palace at the Alhambra. Of less interest are the perimeter towers, including the Mihrab Tower, a former Nasrid oratory; Torre de las Infantas (Tower of the Princesses); and Torre de la Cautiva (Tower of the Captive). Like the Damas tower, these towers were also once sumptuously decorated inside; today only some decoration remains.

Next you can move to the immediate southwest to visit **Emperor Carlos V's Palace (Palacio de Carlos V) ★★**, where the Holy Roman emperor lived. Carlos might have been horrified when he saw a cathedral placed in the middle of the great mosque at Córdoba, but he's also responsible for some architectural confusion in Granada. He did not consider the Nasrid palace grand enough, so in 1526 he ordered Pedro Machuca, a student of Michelangelo, to design him a fitting royal residence. It's quite beautiful, but terribly out of place in such a setting. Carlos financed the palace by levying a tax on the Muslims. In spite of its incongruous location, the final result is one of the purest examples of classical Renaissance architecture in Spain.

The square exterior opens to reveal a magnificent, circular, two-story courtyard that is open to the sky. Inside the palace is the **Museo de la Alhambra ★★** (© **95-822-75-27**), a museum of Hispano-Muslim art with its salons opening onto the Myrtle and Mexuar courts. They display artifacts retrieved from the Alcázar, including fragments of sculpture, as well as unusual braziers and even perfume burners used in the harems. The most outstanding object is a **blue amphora ★** that is 132cm (52 in.) high. It stood for years in the

A staircase in Emperor Carlos V's Palace.

Hall of the Two Sisters. Also look for an ablutions basin dating from the 10th century and adorned with lions chasing stags and an ibex. The museum is open mid-October to mid-March Sunday to Tuesday 8:30am to 2:30pm, Wednesday to Saturday 8:30am to 6pm; from mid-March to mid-October Sunday to Tuesday 8:30am to 2:30pm, Wednesday to Saturday 8:30am to 8pm.

Before leaving the Alhambra precincts, try to see the **Alcazaba ★**, which dates from the 9th century and is the oldest part of the complex. This rugged fortress from the Middle Ages was built for defensive purposes. For a spectacular **view,** climb the **Torre de la Vela (Watchtower) ★**. You look into the lower town onto Plaza Nueva, and you can also see the Sierra Nevada in the distance. From the tower you can also view the Generalife (see below) and the "Gypsy hill" of Sacromonte.

Exit from the Alhambra via the Puerta de la Justicia, and then circumnavigate the Alhambra's southern foundations until you reach the gardens of the summer palace, where Paseo de los Cipreses quickly leads you to the main building of the **Generalife ★★**, built in the 13th century to overlook the Alhambra and set on 30 lush hectares (74 acres). The sultans used to spend their summers in this palace (pronounced Heh-neh-rah-*lee*-feh), safely locked away with their harems.

walking **TO THE ALHAMBRA**

Many visitors opt to take a taxi or the bus to the Alhambra, but some hardy souls enjoy the uphill climb from Plaza Nueva. (Signs indicate the winding roads and the steps that lead to the Alhambra.) If you decide to walk, enter the Alhambra via the Cuesta de Gomérez, which, although steep, is the quickest and shortest pedestrian route. It begins at the Plaza Nueva and goes steeply uphill to the Puerta de las Granadas, the first of two gates to the Alhambra. The second, another 183m (600 ft.) uphill, is the Puerta de la Justicia, which 90% of visitors use. *Caution:* Beware of self-styled guides milling around the parking lot, as they are more interested in separating you and your euros than in providing any real guidance.

Don't expect an Alhambra in miniature: The Generalife was always meant to be a retreat, even from the splendors of the Alhambra. Lying north of the Alhambra, this country estate of the Nasrid emirs was begun in the 13th century, but the palace and gardens have been much altered over the years. The palace is mainly noted for its beautiful courtyards, including **Patio de Polo ★**, where the visitors of yore would arrive on horseback.

The highlight of the Generalife is its **gardens ★★★**. Originally, they contained orchards and pastures for domestic animals. Of special note is **Escalera del Agua (the Water Staircase) ★**, with water flowing gently down. An enclosed Oriental garden, **Patio de la Acequía ★**, was constructed around a long pool, with rows of water jets making graceful arches above it. The **Patio de la Sultana ★** (also known as the Patio de los Cipreses) was the secret rendezvous point

Granada's Baños Arabes.

for Zoraxda, wife of Sultan Abu Hasan, and her lover, the chief of the Abencerrajes.

Palacio de Carlos V. ✆ **90-244-12-21.** www.alhambra-patro nato.es. Comprehensive ticket, including Alhambra and Generalife, 14€; Museo de la Alhambra free; garden visits 7€; illuminated visits 14€. Oct 15–Mar 14 daily 8:30am–6pm, floodlit visits Fri–Sat 8–9:30pm; Mar 15–Oct 14 daily 8:30am–8pm, floodlit visits Fri–Sat 10–11:30pm. Bus: 30 or 32.

Baños Arabes ★ LANDMARK   It's remarkable that these 11th-century "baths of the walnut tree," as they were known by the Moors, escaped destruction during the reign of the Reyes Católicos (Fernando and Isabel). Among the oldest buildings still standing in Granada, and among the best-preserved Muslim baths in Spain, they predate the Alhambra. Many of the stones used in their construction show the signs of Visigothic and Roman carving, especially the capitals. Carrera del Darro 31. ✆ **95-802-78-00.** Free admission. Tues–Sat 9am–2:30pm. Bus: 31 or 32.

Catedral and Capilla Real ★★ CATHEDRAL This richly ornate Renaissance cathedral with its spectacular altar is one of the country's architectural highlights, acclaimed for its beautiful facade and gold-and-white interior. It was begun in 1521 and completed in 1714. Behind the cathedral (entered separately) is the Flamboyant Gothic **Royal Chapel ★★**, where the remains of Isabel and Fernando lie. It was their wish to be buried in recaptured Granada, not Castilla or Aragón. The coffins are remarkably tiny—a reminder of how short they must have been. Accenting the tombs is a wrought-iron grille, itself a masterpiece. Occupying much larger tombs are the remains of their daughter, Juana la Loca (the Mad), and her husband, Felipe el Hermoso (the Handsome). In the sacristy, you can view Isabel's personal **art collection ★★**, including works by Rogier van der Weyden and various Spanish and Italian masters such as Botticelli.

Plaza de la Lonja, Gran Via de Colón, 5. Catedral © **95-822-29-59.** 4€. Mon–Sat 10:45am–1:15pm and 4–7:45pm; closes 6:45pm in winter. Capilla Real © **95-822-78-48.** 4€. Summer Mon–Sat 10:15am–1:30pm and 4–7:30pm, Sun 11am–1:30pm and 4–7:30pm; winter Mon–Sat 10:15am–1:30pm and 3:30–6:30pm, Sun 11am–1:30pm and 3:30–6:30pm. Bus: 6, 9, or 11.

Sacromonte ★ NEIGHBORHOOD   Hundreds of Gypsies once lived on the "Holy Mountain" on the outskirts of Granada above the Albaicín. The mountain was named for the Christians martyred here and for its long-ago role as a pilgrimage site. Many of the caves were heavily damaged by rain in 1962, forcing most occupants to seek shelter elsewhere. Nearly all the Gypsies remaining are in one way or another involved with tourism. (Some don't even live here—they commute from modern apartments in the city.)

You can walk uphill, but you might want to save time by taking a bus or taxi, and you should definitely use a bus or taxi after dark. The best way to see some of the caves and to actually learn something about

Inside a Gypsy cave in Sacromonte.

Gypsy Granada is to visit the **Museo Cuevas del Sacromonte ★**, Barranco de los Negros (© **95-821-51-20;** www.sacromontegranada.com). This interpretation center is a great source of Roma (Gypsy) pride. Several caves are shown as lodgings while others are set up as studios for traditional weaving, pottery, basketry, and metalwork. The museum is open mid-March to mid-October daily 10am to 8pm, mid-October to mid-March daily 10am to 6pm. Admission is 5€, take bus 35 to get here.

In the evenings, many caves become performance venues for the Granada Gypsy flamenco style known as *zambra*. Performances demonstrate varying degrees of authenticity and artistry, but one of the best is presented at **Venta El Gallo, Barranco** Los Negros 5, (© **95-822-84-76;** www.ventaelgallo.com). A *zambra* performance has three stages, corresponding to the three parts of a Gypsy wedding. It is an atmospheric evening that you will not soon forget, but expect a certain amount of ostentatious showmanship for the benefit of tourists and attempts to sell you overpriced drinks. Make your reservation for the show without dinner (unless you feel you have to sit in front), but do pay the extra charge for transportation via minibus because city buses stop running at 11pm, when the musicians and dancers will just be hitting their stride. Admission is 27€, with an additional 6€ for transportation. Dinner and show are 58€.

Monasterio de la Cartuja ★ MONASTERY   This 16th-century monastery, off the Albaicín on the outskirts of Granada, is sometimes called the "Christian answer to the Alhambra" because of its ornate stucco and marble and the baroque Churrigueresque fantasy in the sacristy. Its most notable paintings are by Bocanegra, its outstanding sculpture by Mora. The church of this Carthusian monastery was decorated with baroque stucco in the 17th century, and its 18th-century sacristy is an excellent example of latter-day baroque style. Sometimes one of the Carthusian monks will take you on a guided tour.

Paseo de Cartujar s/n. ⓒ **95-820-19-32.** Admission 3.50€. Apr–Oct daily 10am–1pm and 4–8pm; Nov–Mar daily 10am–1pm and 3–6pm. Bus: 8 from cathedral.

Shopping

Alcaicería, once the Moorish silk market, is next to the cathedral in the lower city. The narrow streets of this rebuilt village of shops are filled with vendors selling the arts and crafts of Granada province. For the souvenir hunter, the Alcaicería offers a good assortment of tiles, castanets, and wire figures of Don Quijote chasing windmills. Lots of Spanish jewelry can be found here. For the window-shopper in particular, it makes a pleasant stroll. A more interesting shopping experience is found in the souk of the alleyways of **Calderería Vieja** and **Calderería Nueva,** where wall hangings, pillows, silk tassels, and silver teapots abound. The area is a low-key version of what you'd find in North Africa, and a certain amount of bargaining is not only permitted—it's expected.

Handicrafts stores virtually line the main shopping arteries, especially those centered on Puerta Real, including Gran Vía de Colón, Reyes Católicos, and Angel Ganivet. For the best selection of antiques stores, mainly selling furnishings of Andalucía, browse the shops along Cuesta de Elvira.

Granada After Dark

Watching the sun set from the **Mirador San Nicolás** (p. 74) is one of the special experiences in this city. But once you have seen the Alhambra glow from the reflected light, the night will still be young.

If you enjoy tapas-hopping, Granada is your city. Its bars usually offer the most generous tapas we have encountered anywhere in Spain. One of the most popular tapas bars is **El Agua Casa de Vinos,** Placeta de Algibe de Trillo, 7 (© **95-822-43-46**), a lively place with an adjoining restaurant.

Another historic spot with a lovely patio is **Pilar del Toro,** Calle Hospital de Santa Ana, 12 (© **95-822-54-70**), near the cathedral and Plaza Nueva. After a few stops, you may find that you don't need dinner. In that case, you can consider an evening of flamenco.

For a performance of Gypsy-style flamenco in the Sacromonte caves, see **Venta El Gallo** (p. 84). We also recommend the sporadic performances (usually on Thurs nights Feb–July) at the **Peña de Arte Flamenco**

la Platería, Placeta de Toqueros, 7 (© **95-821-06-50;** www.laplateria.org.es), the oldest flamenco enthusiasts' club in Spain. The setting is a bit like a church hall, but it's a great place to join real fans and see rising stars. Admission is 10€.

One of the most popular discos is **Granada 10,** Calle Carcel Baja, 10 (© **95-822-40-01**), which opens at midnight daily and doesn't close until at least 6am. Cover charge of 12€ includes the first drink.

Side Trip to Ubeda ★★

Less than 2 hours from Granada by car and a little longer by bus, the Renaissance city of Ubeda could not be more different in demeanor or atmosphere. Granada is the ultimate Moorish city, but Ubeda is filled with Spain's finest Renaissance architecture; it's often called often called the "Florence of Andalucía." The most striking buildings are the work of Andrés de Vandelvira, who created his own vernacular interpretation of the "new" style of Italy. It didn't hurt that his patrons were flush from royal monopolies on the olive oil and wool trade granted by Carlos V (at the cost of a revolt among the nobles of Castilla). The best way to discover the charms of this World Heritage Site is to wander its narrow cobblestone streets and admire the golden-brown Renaissance palaces and tile-roofed whitewashed houses. Definitely allow time for a stroll through Ubeda's shops, which specialize in leather craft goods, esparto grass weaving, and distinctive artisanal olive oils.

The easiest way to visit Ubeda is to take one of the 10 **buses** per day from Granada. They take 2 to 3 hours and cost 13€ each way. For information, call Alsa at © **95-375-21-57,** or visit www.alsa.es. The Ubeda bus station is on Calle San José in the new part of the city; signs will point to a downhill walk to the Zona

Monumental. To drive here, take the E-902/A-44 north from Granada; at Jaen, follow the A-316 spur northeast. When you arrive, you can pick up a walking map at the **tourist information office,** Calle Baja del Marqués, 4 (✆ **95-377-92-04;** www.andalucia.org). It is open Monday to Friday 9am to 7:30pm, Saturday and Sunday 9:30am to 3pm.

WHERE TO STAY & DINE IN UBEDA

Parador de Ubeda ★ ANDALUCIAN   Even if you do not plan to stay overnight in Ubeda, you should take a look at this 16th-century palace. Once you have seen the classic central courtyard, you will almost certainly want to enjoy a meal in the dining room, known as the Restaurante Condestable Dávalos. In *parador* style, the menu features classic dishes of the region carefully executed with fresh local ingredients, such as cold soup with almonds, rabbit stew, shoulder of kid, and a savory olive oil ice cream. After you have enjoyed a leisurely meal, you may even want to spend the night. The guest rooms feature high beamed ceilings, traditional furnishings, and tall windows. Many rooms have views of the main plaza. Plaza Vázquez de Molina, s/n. ✆ **95-375-03-45.** www.parador. es. 36 units. 95€–188 double; 115€–241€ suite. Restaurant main courses 16€–24€; daily menu 34€. Daily 1:30–4pm and 8:30–11pm. **Amenities:** Restaurant; bar; free Wi-Fi.

EXPLORING UBEDA

Centrally located **Plaza Vázquez de Molina** ★★ is flanked by several mansions, including Casa de las Cadenas, now the Town Hall. The mansions suffered from neglect for many years but have all been recently restored, including the *parador* (see above) and El Salvador church (below).

Hospital de Santiago ★ CONCERT HALL   On the western edge of town, off Calle del Obispo Coros, stands the Hospital of Santiago, designed by Andrés de Vandelvira and built between 1562 and 1576. It is still in use as a cultural venue, hosting concerts and containing a minor modern art museum. Over the main entryway is a carving of Santiago Matamoros ("St. James the Moorslayer") in a traditional pose on horseback. Note the monumental staircase leading upstairs from the inner patio. The chapel holds some marvelous woodcarvings.

Av. Cristo Rey. ℂ **95-375-08-42.** Free admission. Mon–Fri 10am–2:30pm and 5–9:30pm; Sat–Sun 10am–2:30pm and 6–9:30pm.

4

Sacra Funeraria de El Salvador del Mundo ★★

CHURCH   One of the grandest examples of Spanish Renaissance architecture, this church was designed in 1536 by Diego de Siloé as a family chapel and mausoleum for Francisco de los Cobos, secretary to Carlos V. The richly embellished portal is mere window dressing for the wealth of decoration on the **interior ★** of the

Sacra Funeraria de El Salvador del Mundo.

church, including a **sacristy** ★★ designed by Andrés de Vandelvira with medallions, caryatids, columns shaped like men (*atlantes*), and coffered decorations and ornamentations. The many sculptures and altarpieces and the spectacular rose windows are also of special interest.

Plaza Vásquez de Molina, s/n. ℂ **60-927-99-05.** www.fundacion medinaceli.org. Admission 5€ adults, 4.50€ seniors, 2.50€ children. Mon–Sat 9:30am–2pm and 4–6pm; Sun 11:30am–2pm and 4–7pm.

San Pablo ★ CHURCH This Gothic church in the center of old town is almost as fascinating as the El Salvador (see above). The San Pablo church is famous for its 1511 **south portal** ★ in the Isabelline style, and for its **chapels** ★ decorated with exquisite wrought-iron grilles. Vandelvira himself designed the "Heads of the Dead Chapel," the most stunning. Seek out the richly carved Chapel of Las Mercedes, done in florid Isabelline style.

Plaza 1 de Mayo. ℂ **95-375-06-37.** Free admission. Mon–Sat 7:30–8:39pm; Sun 11:30am–1pm.

Side Trip to the Alpujarra de Granada ★★

No place in Andalucía so retains its Moorish mien as the rustic mountain villages of Granada province on the south flank of the Sierra Nevada. Isolated until the 1950s by poor roads, the architecture echoes Berber houses in northern Morocco. The green valleys and rugged hills terraced with olives and vines are spectacularly scenic. The area is best explored by car; public transit is spotty. The drive is a treat for fans of twisting mountain roads.

LANJARÓN ★

The first town of the Alpujarra that comes up on A-348 is the least typical. Lanjarón is famous all over Spain for water bottled from its springs, and has been a spa town since the Romans. Eight mineral springs bubble up, each with different alleged healing properties. The town revolves around the spa, called the **Balneario de Lanjarón,** Avenida de Madrid, 2. (© **95-877-01-37;** balneariodelanjaron.com; open 9am–2pm and 5–8pm), which was built in 1928. Twice a day, residents and visitors line up in the lobby to fill bottles with water from a flowing spring. The spa makes a relaxing retreat, with services that range from thermal baths to reflexology (11€–56€).

PAMPANEIRA★★

The lowest spot in town is 1,000m (3,281 ft.) above sea level, and every street leads steeply up from there. This village is the tourism and hiking center for the High Alpujarra, and alpine hikers strut up and down the streets with ease. There are a number of small shops selling colorful, shaggy, woven cotton rugs (called *jarapes de Alpujarra*) as well as jewelry and other handicrafts. Two ham producers also sell their wares, and the village even has an artisanal chocolate maker and a gelato outlet.

But the main reason to come here is to hike. Do *not* set out on a trail without first inquiring about trail conditions at the **Punto de Información Parque Natural de Sierra Nevada,** Plaza de la Libertad, s/n. (© **95-876-31-27;** www.nevadensis.com; open Tues–Sat 10am to 2pm and 4 to 6pm, Sun–Mon 10am to 3pm). The center arranges group and privately guided hikes, as well as rock-climbing excursions. Hikers interested in a good afternoon trek are usually encouraged to follow well-marked trails from Pampaneira to the nearby ridgeline villages of Bubión and Capileira. The distance is only about 3km (1.9 mi), with an elevation rise to 1,250m (4,101 ft.) on switchback trails.

If you want to stay overnight in the High Alpujarra, book ahead for the **Hostal Pampaneira,** Avenida de la Alpujarra, 1 (© **95-876-30-02;** www.hostal pampaneira.com). All 15 cozy and simple rooms have televisions and heat—air-conditioning is never needed. The windows offer million-dollar views, but doubles are only 42€ per night with breakfast. Triples are 50€.

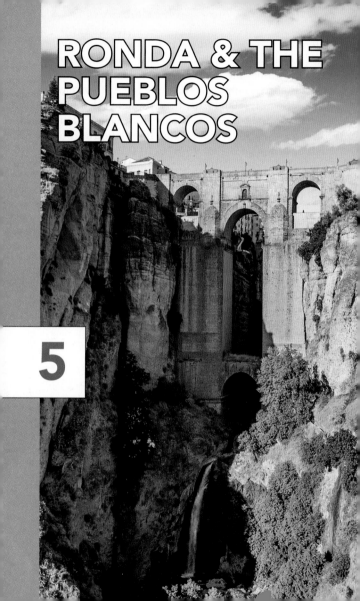

RONDA & THE PUEBLOS BLANCOS

5

Ronda is an incredible sight. The city is literally split in two by the 150m-deep (492-ft.) Río Guadalevin gorge known as *El Tajo,* and houses hang off both sides of the gorge. In 2,000 years, no one has been able to improve on Pliny the Elder's epithet for the city: "the glorious." But, if you are prone to vertigo, Ronda's high eyrie might feel as if the city were built on a spinning plate on a circus clown's pole. Located at the eastern edge of the mountain ridges that separate the Costa del Sol from the Cádiz plain, Ronda is the gateway to the Serranía de Ronda—the serrated ridges that harbored mountain bandits and political rebels from the age of Caesar through the days of Franco. The city is divided into an older part, which is the Moorish and aristocratic quarter, and the newer section on the south bank of the gorge, built principally after the Reconquest. The old quarter is by far the more fascinating; it contains narrow, rough streets and buildings with a marked Moorish influence. (Look for the minarets.)

PREVIOUS PAGE: **Ronda's medieval Puente Nuevo (New Bridge) is the centerpiece of the town.**

Walking in the park in the new section, however, provides some truly extraordinary panoramic views as the pathway follows the edge of the cliff.

Essentials

GETTING THERE   Most visitors take a **train** to the main station at Avenida La Victoria (© **90-242-22-42;** www.renfe.com). Three trains arrive from Granada per day. The trip takes 2½ to 3 hours and costs 20€ one-way. Three trains also arrive daily from Málaga, taking 2 hours and costing 10€. Three trains daily connect Ronda and Madrid. The trip takes 4 hours and costs 73€ one-way.

The main **bus** station is at Plaza Concepción García Redondo s/n (© **90-225-70-25**). There are five buses a day from Sevilla, taking 2½ hours and costing 20€ one-way. There is also service from Málaga, taking 2½ hours and costing 15€ one-way. Also on the Costa del Sol, Marbella runs five buses per day to Ronda, taking 1 hour and costing 14€ one-way.

Major highways circle Ronda, but getting to town requires driving on winding secondary routes. From Sevilla, take N-334 southwest. At El Arahal, continue south along C-339. From Granada, take N-342 west to the junction with N-332, and then take N-332 southwest to the junction with C-339. From Málaga, go northwest on scenic C-344, or from Marbella northwest on C-339.

VISITOR INFORMATION   The **tourist office,** Paseo de Blas Infante s/n (© **95-218-71-19;** www.turismoderonda.es), is open daily 10am to 2pm and 3 to 5pm.

Where to Stay

EXPENSIVE

Parador de Ronda ★★★   You will not forget your first view of this *parador,* which perches practically on the edge of El Tajo gorge. The city hall used to occupy this site, and its facade, complete with clock, was retained in the design of this thoroughly modern lodging. The large rooms have modern furnishings and color schemes in blue, yellow, green, and red. But as stunning and comfortable as the property may be, the city and its environs take center stage here: rooms look out on the gorge or the old city or toward the bullring. Some rooms have a private terrace, but all guests can enjoy the gardens and the public footpath at the edge of El Tajo.

Plaza de España s/n. ✆ **95-287-75-00.** www.parador.es. 79 units. 120€–223€ double; 180€–292€ suite. Parking 22€. **Amenities:** Restaurant; bar; outdoor pool; free Wi-Fi.

MODERATE

Hotel Catalonia Reina Victoria ★   The Victorian architecture of this hotel, built in 1906 by an Englishman, is a surprising change of pace amid Ronda's more traditional Spanish style. A recent and thorough renovation has given the fairly large and airy guest rooms a clean-lined modern feel. But there was no way to improve on the location, amid a lovely garden on the eastern edge of the new town and tucked up close to a 147m (482-ft.) precipice.

Paseo Doctor Fleming, 25. ✆ **95-287-12-40.** www.hotelescatalonia.com 92 units. 86€–170€ double; 130€–205€ suite. Free parking. **Amenities:** Restaurant; bar; outdoor pool; spa; gym; free Wi-Fi.

INEXPENSIVE

Hotel Ronda ★ You can sense the pride of the family that has turned their home into a small lodging. Located just a block from the upper bridge over the gorge, the typical Andalucían-style home features white walls, tile floors, and lots of ironwork. The five simple but comfortable guest rooms are more colorful, with bright-colored accent walls and bedding. Spacious room 5 was once the stable, while smaller room 3 was where the family kept birds. Hotel Ronda is a good option for a tranquil spot close to the action. Guests often take a bottle of wine to the rooftop terrace to enjoy while admiring the views of Ronda's "new town" and the distant Sierra Nieves mountain range.

Ruedo Doña Elvira, 12. ✆ **95-287-22-32.** www.hotelronda.net. 5 rooms. 72€–98€ double. **Amenities:** Roof terrace, access to health club with pool and tennis courts 6km (4mi) from hotel.

Hotel San Gabriel ★★ This enclave of 21 rooms around several patios on a side street in the old city has a timeless elegance. Built in 1736 as a noble mansion, it was converted to a hotel about 20 years ago and is still run by the family that last occupied it as a private home. The interior is rich in detail, with dark wood, stained glass, artwork, antiques, and traditional furnishings that exude character and comfort. The property also boasts a library, a wine cellar for sipping sherry before dinner, and even a small movie theater with red velvet seats rescued from a local theater. Each room has unique decor, but all are fairly spacious.

Calle Marqués de Moctezuma, 19 (just off Calle Armiñán). ✆ **95-219-03-92.** www.hotelsangabriel.com. 21 rooms. 72€–107€ double; 126€–165€ suite. Closed last two weeks of July, last two weeks of December and first week of January. Parking 10€. **Amenities:** Bar; free Wi-Fi in public areas.

Maestranza ★ This modern hotel faces Ronda's bullring, which must have been handy for legendary matador Pedro Romero, who once lived in a villa on the property. While the hotel is one of the more modern in town, it sits behind a classic facade and features restrained, classic decor with dark wood floors and furnishings, offset with pastel colors.

Calle Virgen de la Paz, 26. ℂ **95-218-70-72.** www.hotel maestranza.com. 54 units. 66€–85€ double; 110€–150€ suite. Parking 11€. **Amenities:** Restaurant; bar; free Wi-Fi in public areas.

Where to Eat

Restaurante Casa Santa Pola ★ ANDALUCIAN With six dining rooms spread out over five levels built into the side of the hill overlooking El Tajo near the Puente Novo, Casa Santa Pola is very popular for large groups, business meetings, and even flamenco shows. It also makes a nice special-occasion restaurant, as the kitchen tends to produce big, attractive plates laden with meat. The establishment has stopped calling itself an *asador,* since that implies meat roasted over live coals, but many of the dishes are prepared in 19th-century brick ovens. Best bets are roasts and braises that cook a very long time, such as braised lamb shank or the suckling pig, which is cooked sousvide, then finished in the oven to crisp up the skin.

Cuesta Santo Domingo, 3. ℂ **95-287-92-08.** www.rsantapola. com/es. Main courses 18€–28€; fixed-price menu 38€–60€. Daily 11:30am–5pm and 7:30–11pm.

Restaurante Pedro Romero ★★ ANDALUCIAN Make a reservation if you expect to eat here on the day of a *corrida.* Bullfight fans mob the place on fight days, as it's Ronda's chief fight-themed restaurant, right down to the color photos of matadors and the stuffed bull's head on the wall. Patriarch Tomás Mayo Fernández opened the restaurant in 1971, and he's still there to greet customers, even as a younger generation has taken over the daily operations. The cuisine is more complex than the decor suggest and includes uncommon mountain dishes like partridge in red sauce with butter beans, or duck liver with a sauce of fresh grapes. There's also a surprisingly good selection of fish.

Virgen de la Paz 18. ✆ **95-287-11-10.** www.rpedroromero. com. Main courses 17€–23€; daily menu 18€. Daily 12:30–4pm and 7:30–11pm. Closed Sun night and Mon June–Aug.

TragaTapas ★★ SPANISH The gleaming modern decor and minimalist design make this casual spot the ideal place to try contemporary Spanish cuisine in miniature—and we do mean miniature. Each tapa is little more than a bite, but they're all so good you may find yourself simply trying the whole day's selection as outlined on the blackboard. A single spear of grilled asparagus topped with grated cheese and accompanied by a square of quince paste might seem precious, but it's so tasty you'll want another and another. Pork sliders—a very Spanish variant on the hamburger—are big hits, as is the salmon poached in vanilla and lime juice.

Calle Nueva, 4. ✆ **95-287-72-09.** Tapas 2€–6€, *raciones* 10€–14€. Mon–Sat noon–4pm and 8pm–midnight, Sun noon–4pm.

Tragabuches ★★★ ANDALUCIAN When Tragabuches burst on the scene at the turn of the millennium, it marked the end of the long march of contemporary avant-garde Spanish cuisine from its birth in Basque Country and Catalunya to its conquest of the once-insular gastronomy of Andalucía. Tragabuches continues to innovate and simplify, and eating here lets you bear witness to Spain's culinary revolution. In response to economic hard times, the once astronomically priced tasting menus have been pared back to the level of a special treat. But the same spirit of adventure prevails, with textural contrasts such as yogurt with mint and smoked cod, or foie gras with soft goat cheese and thin slices of tart green apple. The tastes come from Andalucían tradition, but we're pretty sure that no chef's grandmother ever paired shrimp ravioli with an *ajo-blanco* sauce, herring roe, and angel hair pasta.

Calle José Aparicio, 1. ⓒ **95-219-02-91.** www.tragabuches. com. Main courses 22€–32€; tasting menus 58€–86€. Tues–Sat 1:30–3:30pm and 8:30–10:30pm, Sun 1:30–3:30pm. Closed Jan.

Exploring Ronda

The still-functional **Baños Arabes** ★ are among the best-preserved in Spain. They are on Calle Molino de Alarcón, s/n, and are reached from the turnoff to Puente San Miguel. Dating from the 13th century, the baths have glass-roof windows and hump-shaped cupolas. They're open Monday through Saturday 10am to 6pm (winter) and 10am to 7pm (summer), Sunday 10am to 1pm (winter) and 10am to 3pm (summer). Admission is 3€, free for seniors and students, and free for all on Monday.

    Palacio de Mondragón ★, Plaza de Mondragón (ⓒ **95-287-08-18**), was once the 14th-century private home of the Moorish king, Abomelic. But after the Reconquista, it was renovated to receive Fernando and Isabel, who stayed here. The Reyes Católicos had many other more grand dwellings, but few were this charming. Inside you can see a trio of courtyards and a collection of Moorish mosaics. There is also a beautiful carved wooden ceiling. A small museum houses artifacts from regional archaeology. Better than the museum is the restored Mudéjar courtyard where you

prehistoric CAVE PAINTINGS

Near Benaoján, the **Cueva de la Pileta ★★** (© 95-216-73-43; www.cuevadelapileta.org), 25km (16 miles) southwest of Ronda, has been compared to the Caves of Altamira in northern Spain, where prehistoric paintings were discovered toward the end of the 19th century. In a wild area known as the Serranía de Ronda, José Bullón Lobato, grandfather of the present owners, discovered this cave in 1905. More than a mile in length and filled with oddly and beautifully shaped stalagmites and stalactites, the cave also contained five fossilized human skeletons and two animal skeletons.

In the mysterious darkness, **prehistoric paintings** depict animals in yellow, red, black, and ocher, as well as mysterious symbols. One of the highlights of the tour is a trip to the chamber of the fish, which contains a wall painting of a great black seal-like creature about 1m (3¼ ft.) long. This chamber, the innermost heart of the cave, ends in a precipice that drops vertically nearly 75m (246 ft.). Guided visits are limited to 25 people, and the cave is open daily 10am to 1pm and 4 to 6pm. (It closes at 5pm Oct–Mar). Admission, including the hour-long tour, is 8€ adults and 5€ children 5 to 12.

It's easiest to get here by car from Ronda, but you can also take the train to Benaoján. There is no public transportation from the train station, and the walk is 3.5km (just more than 2 miles) uphill. Ronda and the cave are in parallel valleys, separated by a steep range of hills. Driving to the cave requires a rather complicated detour to either the south or the north of Ronda, and then doubling back.

can take in a panoramic view of El Tajo with the Serranía de Ronda looming in the background. Flanked by two Mudéjar towers, the building now has a baroque facade. It's open Monday through Friday from 10am to 6pm (10am–7pm summer), and

Saturday and Sunday 10am to 3pm; admission is 3€, free on Wednesday.

Nearby, the **Casa Palacio del Gigante ★**, Plaza del Gigante, s/n. (© 67-863-14-45; www.turismo deronda.es), was named for the Phoenician stone sculpture in the courtyard. Displays in this small in-town Nasrid palace from the 13th to 15th centuries race through Ronda's formation from the geological forces that created the gorge to the Iberian settlement of the city, the Roman occupation, and then the Moorish urban explosion of the 10th and 11th centuries that shaped the city you see today. The palace has been closed for renovation, but pending funding, should re-open in 2015.

One of the great wonders of Ronda is not that the Romans built the first version of Puente San Miguel at the bottom of the gorge, but that the Puente Nuevo spans the gorge at the top. The **Centro de Interpretación del Puente Nuevo ★★**, Plaza de España, s/n (© **95-287-08-18;** www.turismode ronda.es), tells how it came about. The citizenry successfully petitioned the crown for a new bridge in 1542, but two centuries passed before technology advanced enough to attempt it. The first bridge on this spot opened in 1739—and collapsed in 1741, killing 50 people. The current structure was

Ronda's Plaza de Toros.

begun in 1759 and finally inaugurated in 1793. The interpretation center is located inside the bridge's support structure. Exhibits provide an overview of Ronda's geography and the engineering achievements necessary to construct the bridge. The center is open Monday through Friday 10am to 7pm, Saturday and Sunday 10am to 3pm. Admission is 2€ adults, 1€ seniors and students, free for those under 14.

Ronda has the oldest bullring in Spain. Built in 1785, the **Plaza de Toros ★★** is the setting for the yearly **Corrida Goyesca,** in honor of Ronda native son Pedro Romero, one of the greatest bullfighters of all time and the inspiration for Goya's bullfight etchings and paintings. The matadors all dress in the 18th-century style as depicted by Goya's works. The bullring is a work of architectural beauty, built of limestone with double arches and 136 Tuscan-like columns. The town is still talking about the music video Madonna and entourage staged here in 1994. If you want to know more about Ronda bullfighting, head for the **Museo de la Tauromaquia ★★**, Calle Virgen de la Paz (© **95-287-41-32;** www.rmcr.org), reached through the ring. It's open daily (except days of *corrida*) November through February 10am to 6pm; March and October 10am to 7pm; and April to September 10am to 8pm. Admission is 6.50€, or 8€ with audioguide. Exhibits document the exploits of the noted Romero family. Francesco invented the killing sword and the *muleta,* and his grandson Pedro (1754–1839) killed 5,600 bulls during his 30-year career. Pedro was the inspiration for Goya's famous *Tauromaquia* series. There are also exhibits devoted to Cayetano Ordóñez, the matador immortalized by Hemingway in *The Sun Also Rises.*

Because it was so remote, Ronda became a favorite hideout of bandits in 18th and 19th centuries. The **Museo Bandolero ★**, Calle Armiñan, 65 (ⓒ **95-287-77-85;** www.museobandolero.com), recounts the history and romantic myths of these colorful characters with historic documents and photos, clothing, and weapons. It's open in summer daily from 11am to 8:30pm and in winter daily from 11am to 7pm. Admission is 3.75€ for adults, 2.80€ for seniors and students.

A DRIVING TOUR OF THE PUEBLOS BLANCOS

The brilliantly whitewashed villages and towns of inland southwestern Andalucía are called Pueblos Blancos (white towns) because they cling to their mountaintops like flocks of white birds roosting together. These archetypal towns and villages dot the steep slopes of the mountains extending north from Gibraltar. They occupy that part of Andalucía that lies between the Atlantic in the west and the Mediterranean extending eastward—the land that flamenco musicians refer to as "Entre Dos Aguas," or "between two waters." One of the most traveled routes through the towns is the road that stretches from Ronda to Arcos de la Frontera on the west.

Many towns have "de la Frontera" as part of their name because they once sat on the frontier between Christian and Muslim towns and villages. Although the Catholic troops eventually triumphed, it is often the Moorish influence that makes these towns architecturally interesting, with their labyrinths of narrow, cobblestone streets, their fortress-like walls, and their little whitewashed houses with the characteristic wrought-iron grilles.

The drive outlined below passes by some of the great scenic landscapes of Spain. It skirts thickly wooded areas that are home to some rare botanical species, including the Spanish fir, *Abies pinsap,* which grows in only four locations, all at more than 1,000m (3,281 ft.). As you drive along you'll approach limestone slopes that rise as high as 6,640m (21,785 ft.). Castle ruins and old church bell towers also form part of the landscape. For those who have been to North Africa, much of the landscape of the Pueblos Blancos will evoke the Berber villages of Morocco's Atlas Mountains. The white towns sprawl across the provinces of Málaga and Cádiz, passing south of Sevilla.

The drive is not difficult, but the roads do twist and turn. At points, they climb very steeply to high mountain passes—some of the highest in southern Europe. In practice, this makes the scenic aspect of the drive better for passengers than for the driver, who should rivet attention on the roadway itself. (There are a few scenic overlooks where you can park and look around.)

The ideal time to drive through the Pueblos Blancos is spring, when the wildflowers in the valleys burst into bloom. Fall is also good. Allow at least a day for Ronda (see p. 92). You can pass through the other villages on this tour to admire the life and the architecture and then move on. The best hotels and restaurants along the entire stretch of the Pueblos Blancos are found in Ronda and Arcos de la Frontera. Elsewhere, lodging options and restaurants are very limited, although we have included some recommendations. The drive from Ronda to Arcos de la Frontera can be done in a day, but outdoor enthusiasts should plan a longer stay for hiking, climbing, and even trout-fishing. Zahara and Grazalema can also be reached by bus from Ronda, but not on the same line. Schedules and lines change often. Inquire at the Ronda tourist office.

Zahara de la Sierra ★

From Ronda, take the A-374 northwest, following the signs to Algodonales, a village best known for **Fly Spain,** Calle Sierra 41 (℗ **65-173-67-18;** www.fly spain.co.uk), a first-rate paragliding center. Once you reach Algonadales, head south at the junction with CA-5312 to Zahara de la Sierra, the most perfect of the province's fortified hilltop pueblos. Trip time from Ronda is about 1 hour, and the distance is 51km (32 miles).

Zahara lies in the heart of the **Natural Park Sierra de Grazalema ★★**, a 50,590-hectare (125,000-acre) park. An important reserve for griffon vultures, the park is studded with pine trees and oak forests. The **Parque Natural Information Office** (℗ **95-612-31-14;** www.zaharadelasierra.es) lies at Plaza de Zahara, 3 (the eastern end of the main street). Hours are daily from 9am to 2pm and Monday to Saturday from 4 to

Zahara de la Sierra, as seen from afar.

7pm. It dispenses information and maps for those who would like to hike in the park. There are five major routes, and for most you'll need to seek permission at the office, which also organizes horseback riding, canoeing, and bike trips.

The white village of Zahara itself zigzags up the foot of a rock topped by a reconstructed Nasrid castle. Houses with red-tile roofs huddle around the base of the fortress hill. Count on a 15- to 20-minute climb to reach what was once a 10th-century Muslim fortress built on Roman foundations 511m (1,677 ft.) above sea level. You can visit the castle, which is always open during daylight hours and offers **panoramic views ★** of the surrounding countryside, including the artificial reservoir at the foot of the mountain.

The cobbled main street of the village below, Calle San Juan, links the two most important churches, **San Juan** and **Santa María de la Mesa.** The latter is an 18th-century baroque church worth a look inside (if it's open). It displays an impressive *retablo* with a 16th-century image of the Madonna. The best time to be here is in June for the Corpus Christi celebration (annual dates vary). Streets and walls seem to disappear under a mass of flowers and greenery.

When you leave town heading south on the Carretera de Grazalema, you'll encounter an olive oil press that, despite modern appearances, has been pressing oil since 1755. **El Vínculo** (© **95-612-30-02;** www. molinoelvinculo.com) has displays showing how olive oil is produced from picking to pressing to bottling. In the late fall harvest, you can see the milling; otherwise you can taste and purchase distinctive oils pressed from the Manzanillo and Lechín varieties.

WHERE TO STAY & DINE IN ZAHARA DE LA SIERRA

Arco de la Villa ★ Tugasa, the rural tourism arm of the province of Cádiz, built and maintains this exceptional little stone inn on the west side of the village at the foot of the trail up to the castle. Rooms are spacious if basic. But the beds are comfortable, and the tile bathrooms have modern fixtures and hot water that works. The inn also has a small restaurant, and a cafeteria where you can order simpler (and less expensive) fare. If you want to hike a bit at this great outlook, this is the perfect place to stay.

Camino Nazarí, s/n. ☏ **95-612-32-30.** www.tugasa.com. 17 units. 66€ double. Free parking. **Amenities:** Restaurant; bar; free Wi-Fi in public areas. Cafeteria dishes 4€–9€.

Grazalema ★★

The drive from Zahara to Grazalema is one of the most spectacular in all of Spain, but the roads are narrow and very steep. From Zahara follow the **Carretera de Grazalema,** where the road numbers change often but include CA-9104, CA-5312, and CA-531. You will cross the high point of the mountains at the historic **Puerta de Las Palomas** ★★ (Pass of the Doves). This passage stands at an elevation of 1,356m (4,450 ft.), and the switchback road is a sports car driver's dream. When you reach the junction with the main highway A-372, follow the signs east into Grazalema. This 17km (10 miles) drive will take about a half-hour—much more if you stop for photos.

Most towns of the sierra have Roman origins, but Grazalema was founded in the late 8th century A.D. by Berbers from Saddina, a peaceful lot who chose a green valley over an arid peak and never fortified their town. As a result, Christian and Muslim armies alike passed them by. Grazalema lies deep in a pocket between soaring hills, so it comes as a surprise when you round a turn and first spot it settled in the verdant valley of the Río Guadalete. It is the wettest town in Spain, receiving 2,160mm (85 in) of rain annually, making it more a green town than a White Town.

The small **Municipal Tourist Office,** Plaza de España, 11 (© **95-613-20-73;** www.turismograzalema. info), is open Monday to Friday 10am to 2pm and 4 to 8pm, Saturday and Sunday 10am to 2pm. It hands out hiking trail maps and serves as a clearinghouse for guide services. Its shop sells scarves, shawls, and blankets woven from local lambs' wool in rich shades of brown and beige.

Towering limestone crags overlook the town. For the best panoramic view, climb to a belvedere near the 18th-century chapel of San José. The town has two beautiful old churches, **Iglesia de la Aurora,** on Plaza de España, and the nearby **Iglesia de la Encarnación.** Both date from the 17th century.

Grazalema is also known for its local crafts, especially hand-woven pure wool blankets and rugs. A 5-minute walk from Plaza de España is **Artesanía Textil de Grazalema,** Carretera de Ronda (© **95-613-20-08**). At this small factory, open to the public, you can buy blankets and ponchos that are made from local wool using hand-operated looms and antique machinery. It also sells souvenirs, handicrafts, and traditional gifts. It's open Monday to Friday from 8am to 2pm and 3 to 6:30pm. Closed in August.

The town is also one of the best centers for exploring the **Parque Natural** of the Sierra de Grazalema. For information about walks in the park and horseback riding, see the information office in El Bosque (below).

WHERE TO STAY & EAT IN GRAZALEMA

Villas Turisticas de Grazalema ★★   Built by the provincial tourism agency to encourage family vacations in Grazalema, this little complex of spacious hotel rooms and apartments with one or two bedrooms has split off as a commercial enterprise. The price is still terrific, and the modern apartments even have wood-burning fireplaces with firewood supplied by the hotel. The restaurant at the hotel is known for its local trout dishes. The facility is about a 10-minute walk from the center of Grazalema village but makes a perfect base for a few days of hiking in the natural park.

Carretera Olivar, s/n. ✆ **95-613-22-13.** www.villa-turistica-grazalema.com. 24 rooms, 38 apartments. 42€–72€ doubles; 76€–138€ apartments. **Amenities:** Restaurant; outdoor pool; self-service laundry; free Wi-Fi in common areas.

Cádiz El Chico ★★ ANDALUCIAN   Run by founder Pepe Rojas Gómez and his daughters, this traditional old building on the main square is the best restaurant in town. Rojas was among the first restaurateurs to convince area shepherds to sell him their best lamb and kids instead of shipping the meat to big-city markets. He first made a name for himself among Spanish gastronomes by reviving the region's traditional lamb and kid stews. The restaurant also slow-roasts both animals in a wood-burning brick oven, usually offering the meat with a side of roasted sweet red peppers. This is mountain country cooking at its best.

Plaza de España, 8. ✆ **95-613-20-27.** Main courses 8€–20€. Fixed-price menu 16€. Daily 1–4pm and 8pm–midnight.

El Bosque ★

After the mountain drive from Zahara to Grazalema, the relatively flat westward drive 10km (6.2 miles) through deep forest on A-372 to El Bosque seems like a breeze. Follow signs to **Las Truchas,** which is the combination lodging and restaurant located on Avenida Diputación, s/n (*©* **95-671-60-61;** www.tugasa.com). The facility was completely renovated in early 2014, and provides double, triple, and quadruple rooms for 66€, and suites for 94€. Rooms are basic but clean and include free Wi-Fi in public areas. Nearby you'll also find the visitor information center for access to the **Natural Park Sierra de Grazalema** (*©* **95-672-70-29**) from the western side. (The center at Zahara handles eastern access.) The center is at Calle Federico García Lorca, 1, and is open mid-June to mid-September Tuesday to Saturday 8am to 2pm. During cooler spring and fall days, it is open 10am to 2pm and 4 to 6pm. Even if you don't decide to hike in this area, follow the stream across the road from Las Truchas for a 5- to 10-minute stroll. This icy little waterway is the **Río Majaceite,** the southernmost trout stream in Europe. The stream-side path is often used by local goatherds, so don't be

The hilltop town of Arcos de la Frontera.

Driving Tour Pueblos Blancos

RONDA

surprised if you have to step off the path to let a frisky flock pass.

Arcos de la Frontera ★

Along with Ronda, this old Moorish town is a highlight of the Pueblos Blancos and the site of a top lodging. Now a National Historic Monument, Arcos de la Frontera sprawls along the long slope rising to a sheer cliff. The major attraction here is the village itself, with its Renaissance palaces squeezed onto a medieval Muslim street plan. Wander at leisure and don't worry about skipping a particular monument. Nearly all that interests the casual visitor will be found in the elevated **Medina (old town) ★★**, which towers over the flatlands. The old town gathers inside the crenellated castle walls. Unless you are staying at the *parador* and driving a small vehicle, park your car below and walk up until you reach the site built on a crag overlooking a loop in the Guadalete River.

Plaza del Cabildo ★ is the main square, and the **tourist office,** Calle Cuesta de Belén, 5, (© **95-670-22-64;** www.arcosdelafrontera.es), is open Monday to Saturday 9am to 2pm and 3 to 6pm; Sunday 10am to 2pm. Start your visit at the **Balcón de Arcos** on the Plaza del Cabildo. Don't miss the **view** from this rectangular esplanade overhanging a deep river cleft. You can see the exterior of a Moorish-era castle, but it's privately owned and closed to the public. The main church on this square is **Santa María de la Asunción,** a 13th-century church built atop a mosque that was constructed on the foundations of a 7th-century Latin-Byzantine church. The current facade was last changed in 1732 and bears a blend of Renaissance, Gothic, and baroque styles. The **western**

facade ★, in the Plateresque style, is its most stunning achievement. The interior is a mix of many styles—Plateresque, Gothic, Mudéjar, and baroque. Look for the beautiful star-vaulting and a late Renaissance altarpiece. The church is open Monday to Friday from 10am to 1pm and 4 to 7pm. Admission is 3€.

Down the main street heading out of Plaza del Cabildo is **Iglesia de San Pedro,** with its baroque bell tower. It is on the other side of the cliff and approached through a charming maze of narrow alleys. You can climb the tower, but it has few guardrails and is ill-suited for those prone to vertigo. Paintings here include *Dolorosa* by Pacheco, the tutor of Velázquez, and works by Zurbarán and Ribera. It's open Monday to Saturday from 10:30am to 2pm. Admission is 2€. Continue down Calle Escribianos to the **Convento de las Mercederías,** where the cloistered nuns sell almond cookies at a revolving window in the wall (a *retorno*) weekdays from 10am to 2pm.

WHERE TO STAY IN ARCOS DE LA FRONTERA

Parador Casa del Corregidor ★★   This *parador* occupies the catbird seat in Arcos, holding down one side of the Plaza del Cabildo. Once the headquarters of the king's magistrate, the 18th-century building was completed renovated to make the wing hanging over the cliff into modern hotel rooms with terraces that overlook the fertile plain of the Río Guadalete—the same river that flows from the mountains around Grazalema all the way to El Puerto de Santa María. The few rooms that overlook the Plaza del Cabildo are larger and more old-fashioned, yet are in least demand.

Plaza del Cabildo, s/n. ℰ **95-670-05-00.** www.parador.es. 24 units. 90€–145€ double. Limited free parking on plaza. **Amenities:** Restaurant; bar; free Wi-Fi.

WHERE TO EAT IN ARCOS DE LA FRONTERA

Bar Alcaraván ★ ANDALUCIAN This atmospheric bar sits below the Plaza del Cabildo. In fact, the rooms are actually the vaulted cellars of a palace on the plaza. The menu remains hearty casual food, including regional sausages, fried cuttlefish, baked eggplant stuffed with ham, and stewed octopus. (Arcos has quick road connections to the fishing village of El Puerto de Santa María.) Even on an off night, you're likely to hear a classical guitarist playing. On weekends, there are sometimes flamenco performances.

Calle Nueva 1. ℰ **95-670-33-97.** Tapas and raciones 4€–12€. Daily 1–5pm and 8pm–midnight.

JEREZ DE LA FRONTERA

Like Kentucky with its thoroughbreds and its bourbon, Jerez is defined by its Andalucían horses and its sherry. Just take a walk down pedestrian Calle Larga, and you'll see what we mean. Fashionable young women wear knee-high black boots with tight pants as a nod to the city's equestrian tradition. And the umbrellas on the cafe tables are emblazoned with the logos of Tío Pepe, Don Patricio, or El Gallo instead of the Cruzcampo beer. The soundtrack, naturally enough, is flamenco's quick-paced *bulería*.

Essentials

GETTING THERE   Several airlines offer **flights** to Jerez from Barcelona, Madrid, Palma, Frankfurt, Dusseldorf, and Munich. For details, call ✆ **90-240-47-04,** or visit www.aena-aeropuertos.es. The airport at Carretera Jerez-Sevilla is about 11km (6¾ miles) northeast of the city center (follow the signs to Sevilla). A *cercanía* train runs from the airport to downtown Jerez.

Most visitors arrive by one of 15 **trains** per day from Sevilla, which take an hour and cost 11€ to 26€ one-way. Eleven trains from Madrid also arrive daily; a ticket costs 71€ to 79€, and the trip takes 4 hours. The beautifully tiled Mudéjar Revival train station is a city landmark

PREVIOUS PAGE: **A horse-drawn carriage clip clops through the streets of Jerez de la Frontera.**

on the Plaza de la Estación s/n (© **90-242-22-42;** www.renfe.com), at the eastern end of Calle Medina.

Bus connections are also frequent, and the bus terminal is adjacent to the train station on Calle Cartuja at the corner of Calle Madre de Dios, a 12-minute walk east of the Alcázar.

Jerez lies on the highway (E-5) connecting Sevilla with Cádiz.

VISITOR INFORMATION The **tourist office** is at Plaza del Arenal, s/n. (© **95-633-88-74;** www.turismo jerez.com). It's open October through May Monday to Friday 8:30am to 3pm and 4 to 6:30pm, Saturday and Sunday 9am to 3pm; June, July, and September, it is open Monday to Friday 9am to 3pm and 5 to 7pm, Saturday and Sunday 9am to 2:30pm; in August it is open Monday to Friday 9am to 3pm and 5 to 7pm, Saturday and Sunday 8am to 4pm. Free walking tours depart from the office Monday through Friday at 10am, noon, and 5pm; Saturday at 10am and noon; and Sunday at noon. Note that the discounts with the **Jerez City Pass,** sold mainly in hotels, are not for the Real Ecuestre (see below) but rather for a stud farm outside the city.

Where to Stay

Hotel Bellas Artes ★ Safety is no worry at Bellas Artes, as the regional police headquarters is next door. This refurbished palace is close to the cathedral, and you can study the architecture from the hot tub on the shared rooftop terrace. The high-ceilinged guest rooms with exposed beams and soft pastel decor are downright romantic, but half of them are singles—great for friends traveling together who like their privacy. Two rooms are junior suites, including Room 6 with a small private balcony and stunning cathedral view.

Plaza del Arroyo, 45. © **95-634-84-30.** www.hotelbellasartes. org. 19 rooms. 37€–45€ single; 41€–64€ double; 67€–104€ jr. suite. Amenities: Bar; rooftop terrace with hot tub; free Wi-Fi.

Hotel Casa Grande ★★ The innkeepers at Casa Grande believe in tradition, which is why you'll be given a real metal key to your room instead of a plastic card, and why the small bar is well-stocked with sherry. Many of the 15 rooms circle the central courtyard. They vary in size (some bathrooms are quite small, a few are huge), but all rooms have striking white marble floors, high ceilings, and soothing, low-key traditional furnishings. Room 3, a large superior double, is our favorite. TVs are small, but the Wi-Fi is strong. Guests share a great rooftop terrace.

Plaza de las Angustias, 3. © **95-634-50-70.** www.hotelcasa grande.eu. 15 rooms. 55€–115€ double. Limited free parking. **Amenities:** Bar; free Wi-Fi.

Hotel Villa Jerez ★★ Staying at this boutique hotel north of the old town offers a taste of the the life of the sherry aristocracy. Rooms in the mansion (all except the budget doubles) are spacious and filled with light and look out on terraces, gardens, or the big pool. (The budget rooms are small and in a separate building.) Decor is traditional and elegant with pale walls, classic wooden Spanish furniture, and wrought-iron accents wherever you look. The hotel is plugged into the sherry trade and can easily arrange for private tours of bodegas. The only downside of the Villa Jerez is the 25- to 30-minute walk to Plaza Arenal.

Av. de la Cruz Roja, 7. © **95-615-31-00.** www.villajerez.com. 18 rooms. 65€–115€ double, 113€–140€ jr. suite. Parking free. **Amenities:** Restaurant; bar; free Wi-Fi.

Where to Eat

Bar Juanito ★ SPANISH   Jerezanos will tell you that they never visit the extremely popular Bar Juanito because it's too expensive or too touristic, but every time we've visited, everyone is speaking Andalucían Spanish at the outside patio tables, inside bar, and dining room. You might pay a small premium for the quality of the food and the atmosphere, but it's worth a little extra to enjoy fresh tuna loin salad in sherry vinegar, meatballs in oloroso sherry sauce, or the dark and juicy sweetbreads al Jerez.

Calle Pescadería Viejo, 8–10. ✆ **95-633-48-38.** www.bar-juanito.com. Tapas and *raciones* 4.50€–8€. Open Mon–Sat 1–4:30pm and 9–11:30pm, Sun 1–4:30pm.

El Almacén ★ ANDALUCIAN   Essentially a long, narrow tapas bar with a few tables for sitting, El Almacén features practically every sherry made in Jerez and most made in Sanlúcar and El Puerto de Santa María. Although the tapas include some excellent standards like *patatas bravas,* many choices are on the lighter side and some—like the tempura-fried eggplant with honey—are suitable for vegetarians.

Calle Latorre, 6. ✆ **69-642-69-53.** Tapas 2.50€–9€. Mon–Thurs noon–4:30pm and 8pm–midnight; Fri–Sat noon–12:45am.

La Carboná Restaurante ★★ ANDALUCIAN   This splendid restaurant in what appears to be an old sherry warehouse is really the essence of Jerez. House specialties include big cuts of Cantabrian beef roasted over charcoal and served with a variety of sauces, including a reduction of oloroso sherry. Those same searing flames are used for salmon, hake, and sea bass. Some of the prettiest dishes are presentations of white shrimp from Huelva, *langostinos* (a large prawn) from Sanlúcar, and *carabineros* (scarlet prawns) baked with *oloroso*. Many diners simply opt for the five-course sherry pairing menu, where each course comes with a different glass of sherry.

Calle San Francisco de Paula, 2. ✆ **95-634-74-75.** www.la carbona.com. Main courses 14€–20€; sherry-pairing menu 32€. Wed–Mon 12:30–4:30pm and 8pm–12:30am.

Reino de León Gastrobar ★ ANDALUCIAN Sleek and rather elegant, this Andalucían gastropub features creative twists on classic tapas. The usual tiny casserole of braised oxtail, or *rabo de toro,* is presented as a pressed cube of braised meat topped with rich beef gravy, carrot cream, and dots of green pea cream. Mini-brochettes of Indian spiced chicken bristle from a Lucite block set on a piece of slate. Expect a more hip crowd than at the usual tapas bar.

Calle Latorre, 8. ✆ **95-632-29-15.** www.reinodeleongastrobar. com. Tapas 3.50€–12€. Daily 8am–1am.

Exploring the Area

TOURING THE BODEGAS ★★

If you want to know Jerez, you must first learn sherry. "I was born in Jerez," a tour guide at **Tío Pepe** once told us. "When we are born in the middle of the grapes, we don't drink milk as a child." We figured she was joking, but there's a grain of truth in the jest.

Jerez is not surrounded by vineyards as you might expect. They lie to the north and west in the "Sherry Triangle" marked by Jerez, Sanlúcar de Barrameda, and El Puerto de Santa María (the latter two towns are on the coast). This is where top quality *albariza* soil is

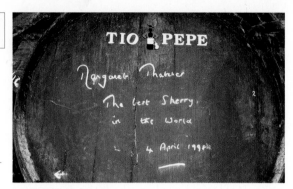

A barrel of Tío Pepe sherry.

found, the highest quality containing an average of 60% chalk, which is ideal for the cultivation of grapes used in sherry production, principally the white Palomino de Jerez.

In and around Jerez there must be more than 100 bodegas where you can tour and taste. On a typical visit you'll be shown through several buildings in which sherry and brandy are manufactured. In one building, you'll see grapes being pressed and sorted (in the fall); in another, the bottling process; in a third, thousands of large oak casks. Then it's on to an attractive bar where various sherries—amber, dark gold, cream, red, sweet, and velvety—can be sampled. Always start with the lightest and driest sherry, either a *fino* or, on the coast, a *manzanilla*. Keep in mind that sherry is much higher in alcohol than table wine.

You have the most choice of bodegas if you visit Monday to Friday. Many of them close during much of August. Here are a few good choices:

One of the most famous names is **González Byass** ★, the maker of Tío Pepe, Calle Manuel María González, 12 (© **95-635-70-00;** www.bodegastio pepe.com). Admission is 13€ (ages 5–18 6.50€). No reservations are required. Tours in English depart Monday to Saturday at noon, 1, 2, and 5pm, and Sunday at noon, 1, and 2pm.

Equally famous is **Alvaro Domecq** ★, Calle Madre de Dios, s/n (© **95-633-96-34;** www.alvaro domecq.com). Tours start Monday to Friday at 10 and 11:30am, and 1pm. The cost is 8€; reservations are recommended.

Lovely and romantic, **Bodegas Tradición** ★★, Plaza Cordobeses, 3 (© **95-616-86-28;** www.bodegas tradicion.com), focuses exclusively on sherries classified as V.O.S. (aged 20 years or more) and V.O.R.S. (aged more than 30 years). The bodega owner has amassed an impressive collection of Spanish art from the 15th to 19th centuries, including a pair of portraits by Goya. Visitors can see some of it in the bodega gallery—a rare glimpse into the world of sherry privilege. Reservations are required, and the visit and tasting cost 20€.

Alcazár ★ FORTRESS   Jerez was a frontier town that went back and forth between Moors and Christians, and this fortress was built in the 12th century as a rural outpost to hold the line against Christian encroachment. It contains an austerely beautiful mosque, lovely gardens, and some of the best-preserved Moorish baths in Andalucía. Although the mosque was converted to a church in 1264, the mihrab, or prayer niche, was preserved—as was the boiler system of the baths, enabling you to see how they operated. The alcázar also functions as a local history museum, displaying two of the ancient olive mills. (In the 1700s, Jerez had 32 active olive mills.) The fortress also contains the Palacio Villavicencio, a noble palace constructed from the late 1600s to 1927. Its history paintings are mostly remarkable for their immense size. A tower room contains a *camera obscura*, which projects images of the city in a darkened room.

Alameda Vieja, s/n. © **95-632-69-23.** www.turismojerez.com. Alcázar only 5€ adults, 1.80€ students and seniors; with camera obscura 7€ adults, 4.20€ students and seniors. Nov–Feb daily 9:30am–3pm; Mar–June & Sept 16–Oct Mon–Fri 9:30am–8pm & Sat–Sun 9:30am–3pm; July–Sep 15 Mon–Fri 9:30am–10pm, Sat–Sun 9:30am–3pm.

Centro Andaluz de Flamenco ★ CULTURAL INSTITUTION

One of the many cradles of flamenco is Jerez, where Moorish, Gypsy, Jewish, and Andalucían traditions met. This academic center possesses the largest public archive of books, musical scores, and performance videos of flamenco in Spain. Flamenco engravings and paintings line the walls of the central courtyard, and free videos are screened in the auditorium. You'll always hear flamenco in the background—the center features recordings by a different artist every week. Staff are steeped in the local scene; ask about upcoming performances at the city's proliferating *tabanco* sherry bars and commercial nightclub *tablaos*.

Plaza de San Juan, 1. © **95-681-41-32.** www.centroandaluzde flamenco.es. Free. Mon–Fri 9am–2pm, Wed 4:30–7pm.

DAY TRIP TO SANLÚCAR DE BARRAMEDA ★

This port where the Rio Guadalquivír meets the Bay of Cádiz may have lost its deep harbor of ages past, but

ay, **CABALLERO!**

Horses have fascinated Spaniards since Neolithic artists painted images of steeds in the caves outside Ronda 20,000 years ago. The museum at the **Fundación Real Escuela Andaluza del Arte Ecuestre,** Avenida Duque de Abrantes, s/n (© **95-631-80-15;** www.realescuela.org), traces the evolving bond between man and beast, emphasizing horsemanship skills and the breeding of the Pura Raza Española, or "pure Spanish race." The top blood lines of what English-speakers call the Andalucían horse were first established at Carthusian monasteries in the late Middle Ages.

The Real Escuela, founded in 1973, trains horses and riders and operates a breeding farm. Performances of the exquisitely trained, so-called "dancing horses" (always Thurs at noon, but also other days depending on the season; 17€–27€) are a great spectacle. Before the show, you can tour the grounds and visit the saddlery and museums of equestrian art and carriages. On non-performance days, you can also visit the facility (Mon, Wed, and Fri, 10am–2pm; 6.50€–11€) and take in the same sights. But the highlight is the chance to watch a practice session. Even during practice, most horses and riders are a polished team. The last time we visited, we watched three trainers encourage a nervous horse to perform the signature chorus-line prances. Every few minutes, the trainers stopped to speak softly to the horse, rub his nose and pat his flanks. It was a revealing glimpse at the hard work, patience, and persistence behind the dazzling artistry.

its sandbars and silted beaches make it a playground of the south. Well-off Spaniards flock here around Easter to bask in the sun, walk or ride horses on the beach, and eat mounds of fresh seafood in the restaurants. Sanlúcar also produces *manzanilla* sherry, a delicate style that can only be obtained by aging in the salt air by the ocean.

The simplest way to get to Sanlúcar from Jerez is to drive the 25km (15 miles) on the A-480. Alternately, buses run every hour between Jerez and Sanlúcar from 7am to 9pm weekdays, every 2 hours 9am to 9pm on weekends. The **tourist office** is at **Calzada de Ejército** s/n (© **95-636-61-10;** www.sanlucarde barrameda.es). It's open Monday to Friday 10am to 2pm and Saturday and Sunday 10am to 2pm and 6 to 8pm.

Sanlúcar's harbor at the mouth of the Guadalquivir was once so deep that Columbus launched his third voyage to America here. But centuries of silting have made the river shallower, creating lovely in-town beaches and protecting the upstream wetlands of Parque Doñana. The healthy estuarine system is a fisherman's delight. Look for extraordinary shrimp, king prawns, and rock lobster on restaurant menus. Most visitors gravitate to the sandy strand at Bajo de Guia or to restaurant-lined Plaza del Cabildo.

When Magellan sailed from Sanlúcar in 1519 to circumnavigate the globe, he reportedly spent more on *manzanilla* than he did on armaments. To understand why, visit one of the *manzanilla* producers. **Bodegas Barbadillo ★**, Calle Sevilla, 1 (© **95-638-55-21;** www.barbadillo.com) has been crafting and aging sherry since 1821. The bodega offers guided tours in English Tuesday to Saturday at 11am, and Sunday at noon. The price per person is 5€, and reservations are recommended.

The marques emblazoned on cafe umbrellas on **Plaza del Cabildo ★** signal who owns each bar. Stop at any one to order a plate of shrimp and glass of *manzanilla* to enjoy in the sunshine.

Visiting Parque Doñana

Parque Doñana ★★ NATURE PRESERVE   Sanlúcar is the departure for boat trips to the marshes at the mouth of the Guadalquivír River. More than merely scenic, they sustain the Bay of Cádiz shellfishery, and were finally recognized in the late 20th century as one of the most important estuary systems in Europe. They literally keep millions of birds alive as they migrate each year between Europe and Africa. The marshes are also rich with resident storks, egrets, herons, and songbirds. The interpretive center at the **Fábrica de Hielo (Ice House)** on Bajo de Guia beach explains the marshes, shifting sands, and stabilized sands of the complex ecosystem. The center books 2½-hour riverboat trips into the park, as well as a combined boat and all-terrain vehicle trip to explore different habitats.

Av. Bajo de Guia s/n. ✆ **95-638-16-35.** www.visitasdonana. com. Visitor center free. Daily 9am–8pm. Two riverboat trips daily in morning and afternoon. Prices from 17€ adults, 12€ students & seniors, 8€ children.

Where to Eat in Sanlúcar de Barrameda

Restaurante Mirador de Doñana ★★ ANDALUCIAN   You can get great shrimp and langostinos at almost any bar in Sanlúcar, but if you really want the top of the catch and the best views while enjoying it, the Mirador is the only choice. Many people are perfectly happy eating outside along the beach or in the indoor dining room, but for the best views, head upstairs where the name "scenic overlook of Doñana" is really true. It can be difficult to sort out the different kinds of shrimp and prawns—not to mention the salt-water crayfish and different forms of lobster—but rest assured, they are all good.

Bajo de Guia. ℂ **95-636-42-05.** www.miradordonana.com. Reservations recommended for best views. Main courses 9€–30€. Open daily 1:30-3:30pm and 7:30–11pm, closed Jan–Feb.

CÁDIZ

7

Residents of this seaport city on the Atlantic coast are a forward-thinking lot, yet they still call themselves Gaditanos, a reference to the Phoenician trading post founded here about 1100 B.C. As Western Europe's oldest continuously inhabited city, Cádiz fell under the successive sway of Athens, Carthage, Rome, and finally the Visigoths and Moors. Most traces of that storied past were obliterated in the 1755 earthquake that also leveled Lisbon. The Cádiz of today was conceived as an Enlightenment city with long, straight boulevards and now-abandoned fortifications to protect the galleons of New World trade that Cádiz monopolized when ships became too big to sail upriver to Sevilla. Its stately pastel buildings seem to bleach in the sun along the seaside *paseos*. Reasons to visit include a thriving local culture, great beaches, vibrant music scene, and wonderful seafood restaurants.

Essentials

GETTING THERE Fifteen daily **trains** arrive from Sevilla (trip time: 2 hr.; 16€–24€ one-way), 12 of them stopping at Jerez de la Frontera and El Puerto de Santa

PREVIOUS PAGE: **A Cadiz streetscape.**

María along the way. The train station is on Avenida del Puerto, Plaza de Sevilla 1 (© **90-242-22-42;** www. renfe.com), on the southeast border of the main port.

Four daily **buses** run from Madrid to Cádiz. Trip time is 8¼ hours and a one-way ticket costs 27€. The bus is operated by **Socibus** (© **90-222-92-92;** www. socibus.es), at Avenida José León de Carranza (N-20). The terminal is on the north side of town, a few blocks west of the main port.

Driving from Sevilla, the A-4 (also called E-5), a toll road, or N-IV, a toll-free road running beside it, will bring you into Cádiz.

VISITOR INFORMATION The Cadiz **city tourist office,** Paseo de Canalejas, s/n (© **95-624-10-01;** www.cadiz.es), is open in the summer Monday to Friday 9am to 7pm, Saturday to Sunday 9am to 5pm; in the winter Monday to Friday 8:30am to 6:30pm, Saturday to Sunday 9am to 5pm. The office hands out a map detailing four color-coded walking routes to maximize your sightseeing time. The office claims Cádiz is the only city in Spain with such routes painted on the sidewalks.

Where to Stay

Hotel Atlántico, Parador de Cádiz ★★★ A government-run *parador* has held down this beautiful spot between Parque Génoves and Playa La Caleta since the system launched in the 1920s. This latest incarnation, which opened in September 2012, is the third try, and it is the charm. Every room has a terrace overlooking the ocean as well as one or two big beds looking out at the sea through a glass wall, a great writing desk behind the headboards of those beds, and wall-to-wall marble bathrooms. The accompanying spa runs the gamut of beauty and wellness treatments for both men and women, and features a series of splendid rooftop pools, again overlooking the ocean. Staying here is a little like booking a room suspended between sea and sky. La Caleta beach is steps away, while the cathedral is about a 15-minute brisk walk through the city.

Avenida Duque de Nájera, 9. © **95-622-69-05.** www.parador. es. 124 rooms. 150€–220€ double. Bus: 1 or 33. Parking: 16€ per day. **Amenities:** Restaurant; bar, concierge; indoor & outdoor pools; spa; free Wi-Fi.

Hotel de Francia y Paris ★ The name might be French, but the rooms are decorated in modern Spanish taste with a sleek, fresh look. Following the 2013 renovation, rooms feature walnut wood furniture, white walls, new hardwood floors, and floor-to-ceiling draperies that accentuate the high ceilings of this late 19th-century building. All-new bathrooms have spacious shower stalls, sink areas with space to lay out toiletries, and bidets. Most rooms hold two twin beds, a small desk, and one or two chairs. The best have small balconies overlooking the plaza, which is busy in the daytime but relatively quiet by evening. If you visit in the spring, request Room 108, which looks out on blooming bitter orange trees. Leave your windows open, and you'll sleep in the perfume of orange blossoms.

Plaza de San Francisco, 6. © **95-621-23-19.** www.hotelfrancia. com. 58€–79€ double. Bus: 1 or 33. **Amenities:** Free Wi-Fi.

Hotel Patagonia Sur ★★ This limestone-facade hotel fits so seamlessly into the old city that only guests who enjoy the ample hot water in the shower would know that it was newly constructed in 2009 rather than being here since the days of Hercules. Of the 16 rooms, the two penthouse rooms with private terraces are the most desirable and cost only a small premium. The 10 standard doubles are a bit snug, but well designed with ample storage and robust Wi-Fi. Location is just about perfect for walking around Cádiz—steps from the cathedral and the docks, a short walk to the museum and the market, about 15 minutes on foot from La Caleta beach.

Calle Cobos, 11. ☏ **85-617-46-47.** www.hotelpatagoniasur.es. 16 units. 65€–113€ double. Bus: 1, 2, or 7. **Amenities:** Cafeteria; bar; free Wi-Fi.

Where to Eat

El Faro ★★★ SEAFOOD/ANDALUCIAN   The El Faro group got its start in the fishing port of El Puerto de Santa María, but even Porteños profess to prefer the Cádiz branch for staying true to the Bay of Cádiz fish cuisine. Golden walls, painted ceramic plates, and handsome dark woodwork give the dining room an elegance that is only enhanced by crystal glassware and an abundance of fresh flowers. Dishes range from a whole sea bass or gilthead bream cooked in a casing of salt to red tuna with eggplant, caramelized onion, and citrus juices. El Faro is also celebrated for its baked rice dishes, including black rice with squid. Almost all dishes are priced according to the market price on any given day.

Calle San Félix, 15. ☏ **95-621-21-88.** www.elfarodecadiz.com. Reservations recommended. Main courses 17€–25€. Daily 1–4pm and 8:30pm–midnight. Bus: 2 or 7.

Terraza Marisquería Joselito ★ SEAFOOD   One of the more traditional shellfish and seafood spots along the port, Joselito serves both in the bar and on its outside patio just a block from the fishing piers. The menu has three categories: shrimp and clams (including shrimp grilled with olive oil or sautéed with lots of garlic), house "stews" (such as veal meatballs or cuttlefish with small fava beans), and fried and grilled fish.

The real treat is grilled fresh tuna landed at Barbete, one of the world's most famous tuna ports a few miles south of Cádiz. All plates come without garnish.

Paseo de Canalejas, s/n. © **95-625-80-86.** Plates 6€–16€. Mon–Fri noon–4pm and 8pm–midnight, Sat–Sun noon–4pm.

Exploring Cádiz

This port city's **seaside promenades** ★★ circle the old town and follow the sometimes turbulent Atlantic Ocean. Strolling along them provides a powerful understanding of the city and its relationship to the sea, on which Cádiz has always relied for its life and its commerce. You can only imagine what the port must have looked like when the harbor was filled with Spanish galleons bound for and returning from the New World.

The southern and western promenades overlook the ocean. Those *paseos* lead to the refreshing public gardens of Cádiz, including **Parque Genovés** ★, with its exotic trees and plants from all over the world.

Cádiz's promenade along the sea.

The adjacent leafy **Alameda Marqués de Comillas** also dates from the 19th century, but is less formal, and therefore more welcoming.

The wide oceanfront sidewalks pass the silent remains of the Cádiz fortifications. They were constructed with good reason. In 1587, Sir Francis Drake attacked the harbor and waylaid the Spanish Armada, and in the 1590s, Anglo-Dutch

A waterfall in the Parque Genovés.

invaders set Cádiz to the torch. The Spanish crown responded by erecting a series of fortifications around the knob of the city. Two remaining forts bracket the cove of La Caleta. At the north end stands **Castillo de Santa Catalina** (© **95-622-63-33;** daily 11am–7:30pm, until 8:30pm July–Aug; free). Built in 1598, it was the port's main citadel for many decades. It now houses some cultural exhibits, but kids prefer clambering along the ramparts. The **Castillo de San Sebastián** (closed until further notice for renovations) on the south side sits on an island reached across a long causeway favored by surf-casters. The beach at the entrance to the causeway glistens with sea glass cast up by the waves.

The cove between the forts is **Playa La Caleta,** one of two European blue-flag beaches within city limits. The other, more extensive strand, is **Playa La Victoria,** about 32.km (2 miles) farther east on

Avenida Fernandez Ladreda. It is best reached by bus 1 (beach route) or bus 7 (central avenue route). Fare is 1.30€. Get off at Plaza Ingenerio La Cierva. This is a good place to join a pickup volleyball game before grabbing a bite at a beachfront snack bar.

Catedral de Cádiz ★ CATHEDRAL The last great cathedral erected in Spain financed by the riches from the New World, this gold-domed baroque church was begun in 1772. Work halted in 1796 and stalled during the Napoleonic invasion. Finally, the citizens of Cádiz finished the cathedral with volunteer labor in 1838. Like the city, it's a model of openness and light. Even the walls are finished in marble. An excellent audioguide in several languages provides exhaustive detail on each point of interest. Perhaps most remarkable is the monumental carved wooden choir from the Carthusian monastery in Jerez. To get a real sense of devotion, don't miss the 390kg (860-lb) all-silver "paso" that is carried through the streets by 12 men on the feast of Corpus Christi in June. Following renovations, the Torre Poniente was reopened in 2014 and offers panoramic views of the city.

Plaza Catedral. ✆ **95-628-61-54.** www.catedraldecadiz.com. Cathedral admission 5€, 3€ seniors and students; Torre Poniente 5€. Mon–Sat 10am–6pm; Sun 1–6:30pm. Bus: L2.

Centro de Interpretacón del Flamenco ★ CULTURAL CENTER If you visited the Museo del Baile Flamenco in Sevilla (p. 39), you should come here to get the rest of the story. This small center focuses more on the singing tradition and guitar forms than on dance. A small room set up like a *taberna* has two interactive video screens that let you sample different styles of singing, guitar, dance, and even piano.

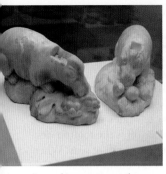

Roman hippo statues at the Museo de Cádiz.

Spend the extra euro for a glass of wine with admission so that you can relax and linger over this rich source of material. Performances are held in this intimate space at least once a week (see "Cádiz After Dark," below).

Calle Santiago, 12. ℰ **95-607-36-77.** Admission 4€; 5€ with glass of wine. Mon–Sat 10am–5pm.

Museo de Cádiz ★★ MUSEUM There's something touching about the two 5th-century B.C. Phoenician sarcophagi in the archaeological collection of this museum. The man's sarcophagus was unearthed in 1887, and when the matching woman's sarcophagus was excavated in 1980, the pair, buried together for eternity, was reunited. In fact, some of the most evocative objects in the archaeological collections are Phoenician—or in the case of the 329 pieces of gold jewelry excavated in 2012, Carthaginian. The ancient jewelry is as advanced in its design and construction as any modern work, and makes an intimate connection to the past. The Roman room is less personal but more monumental, especially the 2.75-m-high (9-ft.) statue of Emperor Trajan excavated near Tarifa in 1980. The fine arts collection on the upper floors is less dramatic.

Plaza de Mina s/n. ℰ **95-620-33-68.** www.museosdeandalucia. es. Admission 1.50€. Mid-Sept to mid-June Tues–Sat 10am–8:30pm; Sun 10am–5pm; from mid-June to mid-Sept Tues–Sat 9am–5pm, Sun 10am–5pm. Bus: L2, 1, 3, 5.

Torre Tavira ★ LANDMARK   In the late 18th century, when Cádiz handled three-quarters of Spain's commerce with the Americas, the city was dotted with 126 watchtowers to monitor the comings and goings of ships in the harbor. The sole survivor is Torre Tavira, erected on the highest lookout point of the old city. Exhibitions on two levels (a chance to pause in the tiring climb of winding stairs) tell tales of the trading heyday of Cádiz, but the real payoff is the rooftop view of the city, its harbor, and the surrounding seas. When you reach the top, you enter a camera obscura with rotating aperture that casts images of the city on the round walls of a viewing chamber as a guide explains what you are seeing.

Calle Marqués Real Tesoro, 10. ℭ **95-621-29-10.** www.torre tavira.com. Admission 6€; seniors & students 5€. Oct–Apr daily 10am–6pm; May–Sept daily 10am–8pm.

Shopping

The **Mercado Central,** Plaza Libertad, s/n (ℭ **95-622-08-60;** www.cadiz.es), is the best place to buy stunning Huelva strawberries in season, bananas and oranges from the Canary Islands, and spices to take home. The market is also ringed by a number of tapas bars. On the plaza out front, **El Melli** (ℭ **95-621-39-33;** elmelli.com) sells an unusually extensive and well-priced selection of flamenco CDs. Two good shopping streets are Calle San Francisco and Calle Compañia. **Spagnolo,** Calle San Francisco, 31 (ℭ **95-607-90-79;** www.spagnolo.com.es), has been creating preppy clothes with a polo theme since before Ralph Lauren was born. **El Potro,** Calle Compañía, 8 (ℭ **95-622-56-73;** www.elpotro.es), the shop of a company based in the leather-working town of Ubrique southeast of Sevilla, has elegant leather goods, and the company's horsehead logo gives many pieces a vaguely Louis Vuitton–like look.

Cádiz After Dark

As in all of Spain, much "nightlife" consists of eating and drinking. For a slightly edgy feel, head to **Taberna Casa Manteca,** Corralón de los Carros, 66 (© **95-621-36-03**), a Barrio La Viña hangout for flamencos, *corrida* aficionados, and lovers of all things pork. The owners are sons of a famous matador, and bullfight memorabilia decorates the walls like religious paintings in a church. The place opens a little before noon and closes when the last patrons stagger out, usually after 2am.

There are two good options for flamenco. **Peña Flamenco Juanito Villar,** Paseo Fernando Quiñones, s/n, at Playa La Caleta (© **95-622-52-90**), is a small, traditionally tiled *taberna* with a stage at one end for flamenco on Friday nights. There's no admission charge, but you're expected to eat and drink. Call after 1pm to reserve a table. The **Centro de Interpretacón del Flamenco** (p. 129) also hosts flamenco performances on Friday nights. The 20€ price includes a light supper and a drink, but unlike the commercial *tablaos,* this is an intimate show for only about 20 people. Both are great choices, with Juanito Villar being a little more free-wheeling and the center more earnest.

At the other end of the cultural spectrum, the Cádiz city government operates **Gran Téatro Falla,** Plaza Fragela, s/n. (© **95-622-08-34;** institucional.

cadiz.es/area/Cultura/35). This imposing 1884 to 1905 neo-Mudéjar brick building presents everything from contemporary and classic theater pieces to star flamenco singers and guitarists, modern dance, opera, and philharmonic orchestras. In May each year, the theater hosts an international music festival of classical music, including the works of Cádiz-born composer Manuel de Falla.

LUNCH TRIP TO EL PUERTO DE SANTA MARÍA ★

The easiest way to get out on the Bay of Cádiz is to take the catamaran ferry, **Muelle Transportes de Maritimo** (*© 90-245-05-50;* www.cmtbc.es), to **El Puerto de Santa María ★**. The deepwater port has a long and storied history. Columbus' flagship, the Santa María, hailed from here, and a plaque on the 12th-century castle in the heart of town honors local mariners who took part in the 1492 journey. Today Santa María is primarily a fishing port filled with small shrimpers, deepwater tuna boats, and headquarters of a number of sherry houses. The 30-minute trip only costs 2.65€, which means that you will have plenty of money left for lunch in this foodie town. Even the father of the current king came here to eat lenguado de fideos at **Bar Guadalete Chico ★**, Calle Micaela Aramburu, 3 (*© 63-734-12-53*). The deceptively simple soup (media ración, 5.50€) is made with fish stock, a touch of tomato, short noodles, and pieces of flounder. People in the sherry trade favor **Bar Casa Paco Ceballos ★**, Ribera del Mariscos, sn (*© 95-654-29-08*), for its tapa of pavía de merluza (2.50€), a long strip of hake breaded and quick-fried in olive oil. Accompany it with a glass of "Bailen," a medium-dry olorosa. Visiting the sherry houses in El Puerto de Santa María requires advance arrangements. One of the most accessible is Osborne, Calle de Moros, s/n (© **95-686-91-00;** www.osborne.es). Tastings and tours range 8€ to 30€, with the top price including tastings of very old, rare sherries.

8

PLANNING
YOUR TRIP

G etting to Spain is relatively easy, especially for those who live in Western Europe or on the East Coast of the United States. If all your documents are in order, you should clear Customs and Immigration smoothly. The staffs of entry ports into Spain usually speak English, and they tend to speed you on your way. In this chapter, you'll find everything you need to plan your trip, from tips on hotels to health care and emergency information.

GETTING THERE
By Plane

FROM NORTH AMERICA   Flights from the U.S. East Coast to Spain take 6 to 7 hours. Spain's national carrier, **Iberia Airlines** (© 800-772-4642; www.iberia.com), has more routes into and within Spain than any other airline. It offers daily nonstop service to Madrid from New York all year, and from Chicago, Boston, and Miami seasonally. Iberia flights are often codeshares with **American Airlines** (© 800-433-7300; www.aa.com), which offers daily nonstop service to Madrid from New York (JFK) and from Miami. Following completion of the U.S. Airways merger, it may offer nonstops from Philadelphia as well.

Iberia's main Spain-based competitor is **Air Europa** (© 011-34-90-240-15-01; www.aireuropa.com),

PREVIOUS PAGE: **The baths of the Alcazar in Seville.**

which offers nonstop service from New York to Madrid and seasonal nonstop flights from Miami to Madrid. Air Europe makes connections from other U.S. cities through its codeshare partner **Delta** (© **800-221-1212;** www.delta.com), which runs daily nonstop service from Atlanta to both Madrid and Barcelona. Direct flights to Madrid depart 5 days a week from New York (JFK). Delta's Dream Vacation department offers independent fly/drive packages, land packages, and escorted bus tours.

FROM THE U.K. AND IRELAND   The airfare market from the U.K. and Ireland is highly volatile. **British Airways** (© **0844-493-0787,** or 800-247-9297 in the U.S.; www.britishairways.com) and **Iberia** (© **0870-609-0500** in London; www.iberia.com) are the two major carriers flying between England and Spain. More than a dozen daily flights, on either British Airways or Iberia, depart from London's Heathrow and Gatwick airports. There are about seven flights a day from London to Madrid and back, and at least six to Barcelona. The Midlands is served by flights from Manchester and Birmingham, two major airports that can also be used by Scottish travelers flying to Spain.

Vueling (© **+44-906-7547-541;** www.vueling.com) offers bargain flights between London Gatwick and several points in Spain. **EasyJet** (www.easyjet.com) flies from several U.K. airports to Madrid, Barcelona, Málaga, and the Balearic Islands. **RyanAir** (www.ryanair.com) flies to Madrid, Barcelona, Girona, Valencia, Sevilla, and Málaga from London Stansted, Dublin, and Shannon.

By Car

Highway approaches to Spain are across France on expressways. The most popular border crossing is near Biarritz, but there are 17 other border stations between

Spain and France. If you plan to visit the north or west of Spain (Galicia), the Hendaye-Irún border is the most convenient frontier crossing. If you're going to Barcelona or Catalunya and along the Levante coast (Valencia), take the expressway in France to Toulouse, then the A-61 to Narbonne, and then the A-9 toward the border crossing at La Junquera. You can also take the RN-20, with a border station at Puigcerdà.

By Train

If you're already in Europe, you might want to go to Spain by train, especially if you have a Eurailpass. Even without a pass, you'll find that the cost of a train ticket is relatively moderate. Rail passengers who visit from Britain or France should reserve couchettes and sleepers far in advance.

For long journeys on Spanish rails, seat reservations are mandatory. For more information call © **91-631-38-00,** or visit www.renfe.com. Fast and comfortable high-speed trains have superseded most other rail travel in Spain. Both first- and second-class fares are sold on Spanish trains. The Spain Rail Pass (see below) is often a practical option if you're traveling largely by rail.

To go from London to Spain by rail, you'll need to transfer stations in Paris to board an express train to Spain.

By Bus

Bus travel to Spain is possible but not popular—it's quite slow. (Service from London will take 24 hours or more.) But coach services do operate regularly from major capitals of Western Europe and, once they're in Spain, usually head for Madrid or Barcelona. The major bus line from London to Spain is **Eurolines Limited** (© **0871-781-8181;** www.nationalexpress.com).

GETTING AROUND
By Plane

By European standards, domestic flights within Spain are relatively inexpensive, and considering the distances within the country, flying between distant points sometimes makes sense. For reservations on Iberia, visit www.iberia.com, or call © 800-772-4642.

If you plan to travel to a number of cities and regions, the Oneworld Visit Europe Pass can be a good deal. Sold only in conjunction with a transatlantic ticket and valid for most airports in Europe, it requires that you choose up to four different cities in advance in the order you'll visit them. Restrictions forbid flying immediately back to the city of departure. Only one change within the preset itinerary is permitted once the ticket is issued. The dates and departure times of the actual flights, however, can be determined or changed without penalty once you arrive in Europe. Costs depend on what kind of ticket you are issued—consult the folks at your transatlantic carrier if you're interested in a multi-stopover ticket and see what the best deal is at the time of your visit. The ticket is valid for up to 60 days after your initial transatlantic arrival in Europe.

By Car

A car offers the greatest flexibility while you're touring, even if you're just doing day trips from Madrid. But don't plan to drive in the congested cities. Rush hour is every hour.

RENTALS All the major international rental car firms maintain offices throughout Spain. These include **Avis** (© 800-331-1084; www.avis.com), **Hertz**

(© **800-654-3001**; www.hertz.com), and **Budget** (© **800-472-3325**; www.budget.com). Tax on car rentals is 15%, so factor it into your travel budget. Prepaid rates don't include taxes, which will be collected at the rental kiosk.

Most rental companies require that drivers be at least 25 years of age and, in some cases, not older than 72. To be able to rent a car, you must have a passport and a valid driver's license; you must also have a valid credit card or a prepaid voucher.

DRIVING RULES Spaniards drive on the right-hand side of the road. Spain's express highways are known as *autopistas,* which charge a toll, and *autovías,* which don't. To exit in Spain, follow the salida (exit) sign, except in Catalunya, where the exit sign says sortida. On most express highways, the speed limit is 120kmph (75 mph). On other roads, speed limits range from 90kmph to 100kmph (56–62 mph). You will see many drivers far exceeding these limits.

If you are fined by the highway patrol (*Guardia Civil de Tráfico*), you must pay on the spot, either to the officer or online using a cellphone and credit card. Penalties for drinking and driving are stiff.

BREAKDOWNS On a major motorway you'll find strategically placed emergency phone boxes. On secondary roads, call for help by asking the operator for the nearest Guardia Civil. The Spanish affiliate of AAA, **Real Automóvil Club de España** (**RACE;** © **90-240-45-45;** www.race.es), provides limited assistance in the event of a breakdown.

GASOLINE (PETROL) Service stations abound on the major arteries of Spain and in such big cities as Madrid and Barcelona. They are open 24 hours a day. On secondary roads, most stations open at 7am daily, closing at 11pm or midnight. All gas is unleaded—*gasolina sin plomo.* Many vehicles run on clean diesel fuel called *Gasoleo A* or on more expensive Biodiesel. We generally rent diesel vehicles for much better gas mileage for a given vehicle size. Fuel prices change often. To check prices and available stations, go to http://geoportalgasolineras.es/.

MAPS   For drivers who don't like or trust GPS, there are still old-fashioned paper maps available. Michelin map 990 (folded version) or map 460 (spiral-bound version) cover Spain and Portugal. **Google Maps** (http://maps.google.com) are extremely accurate in metropolitan areas, but the database is somewhat sketchier on rural roads.

By Train

Spain is crisscrossed with a comprehensive network of rail lines on RENFE the national rail line. High-speed AVE, AVANT, ALVIA, and ALTRIA trains have reduced travel time between Madrid and Sevilla and Madrid and Barcelona to only 2½ hours. Trains are now so fast that few hotel trains are offered, apart from those going to Portugal or France. The RENFE website has possibly the world's easiest-to-use online schedule. Pay close attention to prices on the schedule. AVE trains often cost twice as much as other high-speed trains but are not much faster. Reservations are required on all high-speed trains, even with a discount card or pass, and reservation fees vary depending on the class of train.

JUNIOR AND SENIOR DISCOUNT CARDS   If you are between 14 and 25, you can purchase the Tarjeta Joven Renfe, which gives you a year of purchasing tickets within Spain for a 30% discount regardless of class, type of train, or day of the week. The pass costs 22€ and must be purchased at a RENFE customer service window. Travelers age 60 and older may purchase a Tarjeta Dorada for 6€ at a customer service window. Also good for a year, it provides 40% discounts on AVE and AVANT tickets Monday to Thursday, 25% Friday to Sunday, and 40% every day on MD (*media distancia*) and *cercanías* (commuter rail) trains.

SPANISH RAIL PASSES RENFE offers discounted rail passes that must be purchased before arriving in Spain. In the U.S. and Canada, contact **Rail Europe** (© **877-272-RAIL** [272-7245]; www.raileurope.com).

The **Eurail Spain Pass** entitles you to unlimited rail travel in Spain. It is available for 3 to 10 days of travel within 2 months in either first or second class. For 3 days within 2 months, the cost for an adult is $314 in first class or $252 in second class; for 10 days within 2 months, the charge is $640 in first class or $513 in second class. Children 4 to 11 pay half-fare on any of these discount passes. ***Note:*** This pass must be purchased before arriving in Spain.

The pass works most economically for long-distance travel—the kind of routes you might otherwise fly if trains weren't more convenient and faster (Madrid to Barcelona, for example, or Barcelona to Málaga). The **Eurail Select Pass** for travel in adjoining countries no longer includes France. Talk to a Rail Europe representative for pass solutions that allow rail travel in France as well as Spain.

EURAILPASS AND RAIL PASSES The Eurailpass permits unlimited first-class rail travel in any country in western Europe except the British Isles (good in Ireland). Passes are available for purchase online (www.eurail.com). Purchase passes before you leave home as not all passes are available in Europe; also, passes purchased in Europe will cost more.

The **Eurail Global Pass** allows you unlimited travel in 21 Eurail-affiliated countries. You can travel on any of the days within the validity period, which is available for 15 days, 21 days, 1 month, 2 months, 3 months, and some other possibilities as well. Prices for first-class adult travel start at $810 for 15 days and range up to $2,234 for 3 months. Children 4 to 11 pay half-fare; those 3 and under travel for free. A **Eurail Global Pass Saver,** also valid for first-class travel in 21 countries, offers a 15% discount for two or more people traveling together. *Note:* This pass must be purchased before arriving in Spain.

WHERE TO BUY RAIL PASSES   The main North American supplier is **Rail Europe** (© **877-272-RAIL** [272-7245]; www.raileurope.com), which can also give you informational brochures and counsel you on which passes work best for your circumstances.

Many different rail passes are available in the United Kingdom for travel in Britain and continental Europe. Stop in at the **International Rail Centre,** Victoria Station, London SWIV 1JY (© **0870-5848-848** in the U.K.). Some of the most popular passes, including Inter-Rail and Euro Youth, are offered only to travelers ages 25 and under; these allow unlimited second-class travel through most European countries.

By Bus

Bus service in Spain is low priced and comfortable enough for short journeys. The efficiency of train travel has cut drastically into available bus routes. Almost every bus schedule in Spain is available on the **Movelia** website (www.movelia.es), which also provides a

Hotel Price Code

The following hotel price codes apply for this edition:
Expensive—200€ and up
Moderate—100€–200€
Inexpensive—up to 100€

means for purchasing tickets through the Internet if you have access to a printer.

TIPS ON ACCOMMODATIONS

From castles converted into hotels to modern high-rise resorts overlooking the Mediterranean, Spain has some of the most varied hotel accommodations in the world—with equally varied price ranges. Accommodations are broadly classified as follows:

ONE- TO FIVE-STAR HOTELS   The Spanish government rates hotels by stars, plus the designation "GL" (Grand Luxe) for the most luxurious properties. The star system is not very helpful, since many criteria are based on suitability for business meetings.

HOSTALES   Not to be confused with a youth hostel, a *hostal* is a modest hotel without services. They're often a good buy. You'll know it's a *hostal* if a small s follows the capital letter h on the blue plaque by the door.

YOUTH HOSTELS   Spain has about 140 hostels (*albergues de juventud*) and they are not limited to young people. Some are equipped for persons with disabilities. Many hostels impose an 11pm curfew. For information, contact **Red Española de Alberques Juveniles** (© **91-522-70-07**; www.reaj.com).

PARADORES The Spanish government runs a series of unique state-owned inns called *paradores* that blanket the country. Castles, monasteries, palaces, and other grand buildings have been taken over and converted into hotels. Several newer properties were simply built from scratch to look monumental. To book or learn more contact **Paradores de España (© 90-254-79-79;** www.parador.es). Make reservations directly with the network's website as third-party bookers tend to surcharge reservations. *Paradores* offer good discounts when one of the travelers is under 30 or over 65, or if you purchase 5 nights (which can all be in different *paradores*).

[FastFACTS] SPAIN

Business Hours

Banks are open Monday to Friday 9:30am to 2pm and Saturday 9:30am to 1pm. Most other offices are open Monday to Friday 9am to 5 or 5:30pm; the longtime practice of early closings in summer seems to be dying out. In restaurants, lunch is usually 1 to 4pm and dinner 9 to 11:30pm or midnight. There are no set rules for the opening of bars and taverns; many open at 8am, others at noon. Most stay open until 1:30am or later. Major stores are open Monday to Saturday from 9:30am to 8pm; smaller establishments, however, often take a siesta, doing business 9:30am to 1:30pm and 4:30 to 8pm. Hours can vary from store to store.

Customs

You can bring into Spain most personal effects along with reasonable amounts of alcohol and tobacco products. For sports equipment you are allowed fishing gear, one bicycle, skis, tennis or squash racquets, and golf clubs.

Disabled Travelers

Because of Spain's many hills and endless flights of stairs, visitors with mobility issues may have difficulty getting around the country, but conditions are slowly improving. Newer hotels are more sensitive to the needs of those with disabilities, and the more expensive restaurants, in general, are wheelchair accessible.

Organizations that offer a vast range of resources and assistance to travelers with disabilities include **MossRehab** (© **800-CALL-MOSS** [225-5667]; www. mossresourcenet. org); the **American Foundation for the Blind (AFB;** © **800-232-5463;** www.afb. org); and **SATH** (Society for Accessible Travel & Hospitality; © **212-447-7284;** www.sath.org). **AirAmbulanceCard. com** (© **877-424-7633**) is now partnered with SATH and allows you to preselect top-notch hospitals in case of an emergency.

Many travel agencies offer customized tours and itineraries for travelers with disabilities. Among them are **Flying Wheels Travel** (© **877-451-5006** or 507-451-5005; www.flyingwheels travel.com) and **Accessible Journeys** (© **800-846-4537** or 610-521-0339; www.disability travel.com).

Flying with Disability (www.flying-with-disability.org) is a comprehensive information source on airplane travel.

British travelers should contact **Tourism for All** (© **0845-124-9971** in the U.K. only; www.tourismfor all.org.uk) to access a wide range of travel information and resources for seniors and those with disabilities.

Doctors All hotel front desks keep a list of doctors available in their area; most of them are fluent in English.

Drinking Laws The legal drinking age is 18. Bars, taverns, and cafeterias usually open at 8am, and many serve alcohol to 1:30am or later. Generally, you can purchase alcoholic beverages at almost any market.

Drugstores To find an open pharmacy (*farmacia*) outside normal business hours, check the list of stores posted on the door of any drugstore. The law requires drugstores to operate on a rotating system of hours so that there's always a drugstore open somewhere, even Sunday at midnight.

Electricity The U.S. uses 110-volt electricity, Spain 220-volt. Most low-voltage electronics, such as laptops, iPods, and cellphone chargers, do fine with 220-volt. Spain uses the European standard rounded two-prong plug.

Embassies & Consulates If you lose your passport, fall seriously ill, get into legal trouble, or have some other serious problem, your embassy or consulate can help. These are the Madrid addresses and contact information:

Australia: Torre Espacio, Paseo de la Castellana 259D; ✆ 91-353-66-00; www.spain.embassy.gov.au; **Canada:** Torre Espacio, Paseo de la Castellana 259D; ✆ 91-382-84-00; www.canadainternational.gc.ca; **Ireland:** Paseo de la Castellana 46, Ireland House; ✆ 91-436-40-93; www.irlanda.es; **New Zealand:** Calle Pinar 7, 3rd Floor; ✆ 91-523-02-26; www.nzembassy.com/spain; **United Kingdom:** Torre Espacio, Paseo de la Castellana 259D;

✆ **91-714-63-00;** www.gov.uk/government/world/organisations/british-embassy-madrid; **United States:** Calle Serrano 75; ✆ **91-587-22-00;** http://madrid.usembassy.gov.

Emergencies Call ✆ **112** for fire, police, and ambulance services.

Health Spain should not pose any major health hazards. Tap water is safe to drink. Sushi and sashimi from Atlantic fish are safe to be eaten raw. During the summer, limit your exposure to the sun. Use a sunscreen with a high sun protection factor (SPF) and apply it liberally.

Insurance For information on traveler's insurance, trip cancellation insurance, and medical insurance while traveling, please visit www.frommers.com/tips.

Internet & Wi-Fi Wi-Fi—pronounced "wee-fee" in Spanish—is becoming ubiquitous in Spain. Most lodgings offer free Wi-Fi, at least in public areas. Some hotels give away basic Wi-Fi but charge for faster access. For Wi-Fi on a phone or tablet, download the GOWEX Free Wi-Fi app from the Apple Store. Internet cafes are vanishing, but if you find one, expect to pay 2€ to 4€ per hour.

Language The official language in Spain is Castilian **Spanish** (or *Castellano*). Although Spanish is spoken in every province of Spain, local tongues reasserted themselves with the restoration of democracy in 1975. After years of being outlawed during the Franco dictatorship, **Catalan** has returned to

Barcelona and Catalunya, even appearing on street signs; this language and its derivatives are also spoken in the Valencia area and in the Balearic Islands, including Mallorca (even though natives there will tell you they speak Mallorquín). **Basque** is widely spoken in the Basque region (the northeast, near France). Likewise, **Galego,** which sounds and looks very much like Portuguese, has enjoyed a renaissance in Galicia (the northwest). English is spoken in most hotels, restaurants, and shops.

Legal Aid   In case of trouble with the authorities, contact your local embassy or consulate, which will recommend an English-speaking lawyer in your area. You will, of course, be charged a typical attorney's fee for representation.

LGBT Travelers

In 1978, Spain legalized homosexuality among consenting adults and in 1995 banned discrimination based on sexual orientation. Madrid and Barcelona are major centers of gay life in Spain. The most popular resorts for gay travelers are Sitges (south of Barcelona), Torremolinos, and Ibiza.

Lost & Found

To report a lost credit card, contact the following toll-free in Spain: American Express at ✆ **91-572-03-03;** Diners Club at ✆ **91-547-40-00;** MasterCard at ✆ **90-097-12-31;** or Visa at ✆ **90-099-11-24.**

Mail   Sending a postcard or letter to the U.S. starts at 0.90€. To calculate the price, visit http://correos.es. You can also buy stamps at any place that sells tobacco.

Mobile Phones

You'll likely not be able to use a North American cellphone in Spain unless it's GSM/GPRS-compatible and unless it operates with a SIM card. Virtually all cellphones in Spain operate with this system, as do AT&T and T-Mobile cellphones from North America. Most mobile phones from the U.K. are compatible.

Many travelers opt to simply buy a pre-paid cell phone on location. **Vodafone** (www.vodafone.com); **Movistar** (aka Telefónica, www.movistar.com); **Orange** (www.orange.es); and **Yoigo** (www.yoigo.com) are the four largest and most reliable mobile phone service providers in Spain. Movistar is the oldest and most established.

Money & Costs

Many prices for children—generally defined as ages 6 to 17—are lower than for adults. Fees for children 5 and under are generally waived. Admission prices for seniors (over 60, 62, or 65, depending on venue) are the same as for children. Exchange enough petty cash to cover airport incidentals, tipping, and transportation to your hotel before you leave home, or withdraw money upon arrival at an airport ATM. Best exchange rates are usually from ATMs. Avoid exchanging money at commercial exchange bureaus and hotels, which generally have the highest transaction fees.

Newspapers & Magazines
All cities and towns, of course, have Spanish-language newspapers and magazines. However, in the tourist areas of big cities, many kiosks sell editions of the *International*

New York Times along with *Time*.

Safety
Spain has not been targeted by jihadists since 2004 and Basque nationalists have foresworn violence. U.S. State Department's Worldwide Caution public announcements are available at http://travel.state.gov, but take them with a grain of salt, as the same conditions that prompt a travel advisory are everyday realities in most American cities and towns.

Spain's crime rate more closely resembles Canada's than the U.S. That said, muggings and robberies do occur, so be careful. Stay out of dark alleys and don't go off with strangers. Exercise caution by carrying limited cash and credit cards. Leave extra cash, credit cards, passports, and personal documents in a safe

location. Don't leave anything visible in a parked car. Loss or theft abroad of a passport should be reported immediately to the local police and your nearest embassy or consulate.

Safety can be a concern for women exploring the world on their own. Avoid deserted streets and do not hitchhike. Dress conservatively, especially in remote towns. If you're a victim of catcalls and vulgar suggestions, look straight ahead and just keep walking. If followed, seek out the nearest police officer.

Senior Travel
Major discounts are available to seniors in Spain, including reduced rates on most admissions and reduced fares on public conveyances. Special room rates are also available at the national parador network.

Smoking On January 1, 2006, Spain banned smoking in the workplace, and on January 1, 2011, included restaurants, bars, and nightclubs in the ban. Smoking is also banned on public transportation and in other areas such as cultural centers.

Taxes The internal sales tax (known in Spain as IVA) ranges from 8% to 33%, depending on the commodity being sold. Food, wine, and basic necessities are taxed at 8%; most goods and services (including car rentals), at 18%; luxury items (jewelry, all tobacco, imported liquors), at 33%; and hotels, at 8%.

Telephones To call Spain:

1. Dial the international access code: **011** from the U.S.; 00 from the U.K., Ireland, or New Zealand; or 0011 from Australia.

2. Dial the country code **34.**

3. Dial the city code, and then the number.

To make international calls from Spain, first dial 00 and then the country code (U.S. or Canada 1, U.K. 44, Ireland 353, Australia 61, New Zealand 64). Next dial the area code and number. For example, if you wanted to call the British Embassy in Washington, D.C., you would dial 00-1-202-588-7800.

For directory assistance: Dial ✆ **1003** in Spain.

For operator assistance: If you need operator assistance in making an international call, dial ✆ **025.**

Toll-free numbers: Numbers beginning with **900** in Spain are toll-free.

Time Spain is 6 hours ahead of Eastern Time in the United States.

Daylight saving time is in effect from the last Sunday in March to the last Sunday in September.

Tipping Don't overtip. The government requires that restaurant and hotel bills include their service charges—usually 15% of the bill. However, that doesn't mean you should skip out of a place without dispensing an extra euro or two. Some guidelines:

Your **hotel porter** should get 1€ per bag. **Chambermaids** should be given 1€ per day, more if you're generous. Tip **doormen** 1€ for assisting with baggage and 1€ for calling a cab.

For **cabdrivers,** add about 10% to the fare as shown on the meter. At airports, such as Barajas in Madrid and major terminals, the **porter** who handles your luggage will present you with a fixed-charge bill.

Service is included in restaurant bills, but it is the custom to tip extra—in fact, the **waiter** will expect a tip.

Barbers and **hairdressers** expect a 10% to 15% tip. **Tour guides** expect 2€, although a tip is not mandatory. Theater and bullfight **ushers** get from 1€.

Toilets In Spain they're called *aseos, servicios,* or *lavabos* and are labeled *caballeros* for men and *damas* or *señoras* for women. If you can't find any, go into a bar, but you should order something.

Visas For visits of less than 3 months, visas are not needed for citizens of the U.S., Canada, Ireland, Australia, New Zealand, and the U.K. For information on obtaining a visa, see your consulate or embassy.

Visitor Information The Tourist Office of Spain's official website can be found at **www.spain.info.**

TOURS

It would be impossible for us to list all of the tours that are offered for visitors to Spain. We've limited this list to some of the most well-respected and long-established tours. But do your own research as well; even the most long-running company can experience financial difficulties and go out of business. When purchasing a tour, it's often a good idea to purchase travel insurance from a third party, as tours can be expensive. Don't purchase from the company itself; if it goes belly-up, you'll lose your insurance, too.

Art Tours

Heritage Tours (© **800-378-4555** or 212-206-8400; htprivatetravel.com) offers customized itineraries focusing on art and architecture. Founded by architect Joel Zack, these tours can be customized and often include guided trips to Spain's top architectural and artistic sites.

CHANGES IN credit cards

SmartChips are embedded in most European credit cards and in very few cards issued in North America. But merchants in Spain use credit card terminals that read the chips but can also accept a magnetic strip like those used on U.S. cards. You will need a 4-digit PIN to complete the purchase, so get a 4-digit PIN from your credit card's issuing bank before leaving home, or call the number on the back of each card and ask for one. Your American Express card will work where an Amex logo is displayed, but it is not as widely accepted as Visa and MasterCard. Of course, you could make sure you have enough cash to cover your purchase.

Featuring groups ranging in size from 15 to 25 participants, **ACE Cultural Tours** (✆ **01223-835055;** www. aceculturaltours.co.uk) in Cambridge, England, offers tours led by an art historian to Moorish Spain or other walking tour options. **G Adventures** (www.gadventures. com) offers excellent Andalucian itineraries, exploring all the highlights of the region plus Madrid and Toledo. Its tours are limited to 12 participants and make use of locally owned guest houses, keeping costs reasonable.

Biking Tours

A leading U.S.-based outfitter is **Easy Rider Tours** (✆ **800-488-8332** or 978-463-6955; www.easyrider tours.com). Their tours average between 48km and 81km (30–50 miles) a day; the most appealing tour follows the route trod by medieval pilgrims on their way to Santiago. The bike tours offered by **Backroads** (✆ **800-462-2848** or 510-527-1555; www.backroads.

com), take you from Seville to Granada, using top-quality inns and expert guides. You'll enjoy the top notch meals, too. **Cyclevents** (www.cyclevents.com) offers a number of affordable, self-guided itineraries throughout the Spanish countryside.

Bravo Bike (© 91-758-29-45; www.bravobike. com) is a travel agency featuring organized cycling tours around Madrid. They have branched out to include other parts of Spain as well, notably the route from Salamanca to Santiago de Compostela. One of the most intriguing bike tours is the *ruta de vino* (the wine route) in La Rioja country.

In England, the **Cyclists' Touring Club** (© 0844-736-8450; www.ctc.org.uk), charges 39€ a year for membership; part of the fee covers information and suggested cycling routes through Spain and dozens of other countries.

Hiking & Walking Tours

Several firms offer guided hiking on the Camino de Santiago across the north of Spain, but **Spanish Steps** (©877-787-WALK [9255]; www.spanishsteps.com) offers the most comprehensive program of walks in terms of number of days and level of difficulty. **Backroads** (see "Biking Tours" above) also offers some of the most deluxe walk tours in Spain, complete with Parador stays, expert historical guides and multi-course meals at top-rated restaurants.

Food & Wine Trips

Spain Taste offers excellent food and wine tours in Catalunya designed for serious gastronomes. They include dinners at Michelin-starred restaurants, wine tastings, and cooking lessons with famous chefs. Tours are conducted from March to June and from September to October. For more information, contact Spain Taste (✆ **93-847-51-15**; www.spaintaste.com).

   Catavino offers 5-day gastronomic vacations which place participants in the quaint Andalucian town of La Sierra de Arecena. From there participants visit nearby farms, bakeries, restaurants and pueblos, cooking each day using only locally-sourced ingredients. The cost for the adventure is 1660€ per person and includes everything. For complete information, go to http://catavino.net.

Escorted General-Interest Tours

Escorted tours are structured group tours, with a group leader. The price usually includes everything from airfare to hotels, meals, tours, admission costs, and local transportation. Escorted tours—whether they're navigated by bus, motorcoach, train, or boat— let travelers sit back and enjoy the trip without having to drive or worry about details. They take you to the maximum number of sights in the minimum amount of time with the least amount of hassle. They're convenient for people with limited mobility.

   On the downside, you'll have little opportunity for serendipitous interactions with locals and cannot deviate from the schedule and itinerary. The tours can often focus on the heavily visited sites, so you miss out on many lesser-known attractions.

   A number of companies are beginning to offer pre-planned tours for individual travelers rather than groups. Some of the most expensive and luxurious independent tours to Spain's major cities are offered by **Abercrombie & Kent** (✆ **888-611-4711**; www. abercrombiekent.com). Guests stay in fine hotels and are welcomed by knowledgeable local guides. **Tauck Tours** (www.tauck.com) offers similarly deluxe tours.

Trafalgar Tours (© 866-544-4434; www.trafalgartours.com) offers a number of tours of Spain. One of the most popular offerings is a 16-day trip called "The Best of Spain." **Escapade Vacations** (© 800-356-24-05; www.escapadevacations.com) sells both escorted and package tours to Spain. It can book you on bus tours as well as land and air packages. It offers some culinary holidays as well as general sightseeing, and can set you up for fly-drive tours on your own. Other companies that offer Spain itineraries include **GoAhead Tours** (www.goaheadtours.com), **Globus** (www.globusjourneys.com), and **Insight Vacations** (www.insightvacations.com).

USEFUL TERMS & PHRASES

9

Most Spaniards are very patient with foreigners who try to speak their language. That said, you might encounter several difficult regional languages and dialects in Spain: In Catalonia, they speak **Catalan** (the most widely spoken non-national language in Europe); in the Basque Country, they speak **Euskera;** in Galicia, you'll hear **Gallego.** However, Castilian Spanish (**Castellano,** or simply **Español**) is understood everywhere; for that reason, we've included a list of simple words and phrases in Spanish to help you get by.

BASIC WORDS & PHRASES

English	Spanish	Pronunciation
Good day	Buenos días	*bweh*-nohs *dee*-ahs
How are you?	¿Cómo está?	*koh*-moh es-*tah*
Very well	Muy bien	*mwee* byehn
Thank you	Gracias	*grah*-syahs
You're welcome	De nada	deh *nah*-dah
Goodbye	Adiós	ah-*dyohs*
Please	Por favor	pohr fah-*vohr*
Yes	Sí	see
No	No	noh
Excuse me	Perdóneme	pehr-*doh*-neh-meh
Give me	Déme	*deh*-meh
Where is . . . ?	¿Dónde está . . . ?	*dohn*-deh es-*tah*
the station	la estación	lah es-tah-*syohn*
a hotel	un hotel	oon oh-*tel*
a gas station	una gasolinera	*oo*-nah gah-so-lee-*neh*-rah
a restaurant	un restaurante	oon res-tow-*rahn*-teh
the toilet	el baño	el *bah*-nyoh
a good doctor	un buen médico	oon bwehn *meh*-dee-coh
the road to . . .	el camino a/ hacia . . .	el cah-*mee*-noh ah/*ah*-syah
To the right	A la derecha	ah lah deh-*reh*-chah
To the left	A la izquierda	ah lah ees-*kyehr*-dah
Straight ahead	Derecho	deh-*reh*-choh

9

USEFUL TERMS & PHRASES | Basic Words & Phrases

168

English	Spanish	Pronunciation
I would like	Quisiera	**kee-syeh-rah**
I want . . .	Quiero . . .	**kyeh-roh**
to eat	comer	**ko-mehr**
a room	una habitación	**oo-nah ah-bee-tah-syohn**
Do you have . . . ?	¿Tiene usted . . . ?	**tyeh-neh oo-sted**
a book	un libro	**oon lee-broh**
a dictionary	un diccionario	**oon deek-syoh-na-ryo**
How much is it?	¿Cuánto cuesta?	**kwahn-toh kwehs-tah**
When?	¿Cuándo?	**kwahn-doh**
What?	¿Qué?	**keh**
There is (Is there . . . ?)	(¿)Hay (. . . ?)	**aye**
What is there?	¿Qué hay?	**keh aye**
Yesterday	Ayer	**ah-yehr**
Today	Hoy	**oy**
Tomorrow	Mañana	**mah-nyah-nah**
Good	Bueno	**bweh-noh**
Bad	Malo	**mah-loh**
Better (Best)	(Lo) Mejor	**(loh) meh-hor**
More	Más	**mahs**
Less	Menos	**meh-nohs**
No smoking	Se prohibe fumar	**seh proh-ee-beh foo-mahr**
Postcard	Tarjeta postal	**tar-heh-tah pohs-tahl**
Insect repellent	Repelente contra insectos	**reh-peh-lehn-teh cohn-trah een-sehk-tohs**
Do you speak English?	¿Habla usted inglés?	**ah-blah oo-sted een-glehs**

English	Spanish	Pronunciation
Is there anyone here who speaks English?	¿Hay alguien aquí que hable inglés?	**aye** *ahl-*gyehn **ah-***kee* keh *ah-*bleh een-*glehs*
I speak a little Spanish.	Hablo un poco de español.	*ah-*bloh oon *poh-*koh deh es-pah-*nyol*
I don't understand Spanish very well.	No (lo) entiendo muy bien el español.	noh (loh) ehn-*tyehn-*doh mwee byehn el es-pah-*nyol*
The meal is good.	Me gusta la comida.	meh *goo-*stah lah koh-*mee-*dah
What time is it?	¿Qué hora es?	keh *oh-*rah es
May I see your menu?	¿Puedo ver el menú (la carta)?	*pweh-*do vehr el meh-*noo* (lah *car-*tah)
The check, please.	La cuenta por favor.	lah *kwehn-*tah pohr fah-*vohr*
What do I owe you?	¿Cuánto le debo?	*kwahn-*toh leh *deh-*boh
What did you say? (Colloquial)	¿Mande?	*mahn-*deh
What did you say? (Formal)	¿Cómo?	*koh-*moh
Do you accept traveler's checks?	¿Acepta usted cheques de viajero?	ah-*sehp-*tah oo-*sted* *cheh-*kehs deh byah-*heh-*roh

NUMBERS

English	Spanish	Pronunciation
1	uno	*oo-*noh
2	dos	dohs
3	tres	trehs
4	cuatro	*kwah-*troh

English	Spanish	Pronunciation
5	cinco	*seen*-koh
6	seis	says
7	siete	*syeh*-teh
8	ocho	*oh*-choh
9	nueve	*nweh*-beh
10	diez	dyehs
11	once	*ohn*-seh
12	doce	*doh*-seh
13	trece	*treh*-seh
14	catorce	kah-*tohr*-seh
15	quince	*keen*-seh
16	dieciséis	dyeh-see-*says*
17	diecisiete	dyeh-see-*syeh*-teh
18	dieciocho	dyeh-see-*oh*-choh
19	diecinueve	dyeh-see-*nweh*-beh
20	veinte	*bayn*-teh
30	treinta	*trayn*-tah
40	cuarenta	kwah-*rehn*-tah
50	cincuenta	seen-*kwehn*-tah
60	sesenta	seh-*sehn*-tah
70	setenta	seh-*tehn*-tah
80	ochenta	oh-*chehn*-tah
90	noventa	noh-*behn*-tah
100	cien	*syehn*
200	doscientos	doh-*syehn*-tohs
500	quinientos	kee-*nyehn*-tos
1,000	mil	meel

TRAVEL TERMS

Aduana Customs

Aeropuerto Airport

Avenida Avenue

Avión Airplane

Aviso Warning

Bus Bus

Calle Street

Cheques de viajeros
Traveler's checks

Correo(s) Mail, or post office

Dinero Money

Embajada Embassy

Embarque Boarding

Entrada Entrance

Equipaje Luggage

Este East

Frontera Border

Hospedaje Inn

Norte North

Oeste West

Pasaje Ticket

Pasaporte Passport

Puerta de salida
Boarding gate

Salida Exit

Tarjeta de embarque
Boarding card

Vuelo Flight

EMERGENCY TERMS

¡Auxilio! Help!

Ambulancia Ambulance

Bomberos Fire brigade

Clínica Clinic

Emergencia Emergency

Enfermo/a Sick

Enfermera Nurse

Farmacia Pharmacy

Fuego/Incendio Fire

Hospital Hospital

Ladrón Thief

Peligroso Dangerous

Policía Police

Médico Doctor

¡Váyase! Go away!

Index